give
yourself
permission

give yourself permission

BE CONFIDENT.
BE HAPPY.
BE YOU.

Cortney McDermott

First edition 2023
Author photo: Alberto Bogo
Editor: Angie Frazier
ISBN: 9781736357019

Library of Congress number: 2023912583

Published by Wisdom House Publishing

*To Dane, for helping me get back up every time I fall.
And to Gaia, the reason I keep getting back up.*

Give Yourself Permission

INTRODUCTION 1

BELIEVE 5

CHANGE YOUR MIND 19

DO WHAT YOU LOVE 35

MAKE A LOT OF MONEY 49

HAVE FUN, PLAY! 63

OPT OUT 79

LIVE BY DESIGN 97

BE CONFIDENT 115

BE HAPPY 131

BE LOVED 147

BE YOU 161

ACKNOWLEDGMENTS 167

Introduction

This book is not about getting somewhere, because you're already there.

It's not about becoming someone, because you already are that someone.

It's not about having or doing, because the having and doing will happen through you once you awaken to the truth of who and what you are.

———

Years back, I started having experiences I could not explain.

Overnight in one instance, I shed considerable weight and my body was visibly toned in ways it had never been before. Another time, I was *transported* out of perceived space-time constraints and merged with a seemingly limitless Intelligence. At one point, I could literally feel the cells of my body and mind reorganizing into a new pattern of consciousness.

Learning was accelerated for me. I knew things, and I couldn't account for how I knew them. Also, time—or my relationship with time—was changing. It was as if I were living lifetimes in a day, so much experience was packed in. Events and situations that would have taken years to manifest were occurring with ease.

If I hadn't personally and spontaneously lived these transformations, I would not have believed them possible without plastic surgery, plant medicine, or science fiction, like the kind you might read in a book or see in a movie. Yet there I was…no surgery, no medicine, no fantasy—proof of the *impossible*.

These experiences deepened my lifelong quest to understand who or what we are, to give myself permission to *not know*, and to play with opening my awareness to new possibilities.

People often ask me how I look younger and healthier every time they see me. They want to know what foods I eat, where I go to the gym, which meditations I listen to. They are looking for a recipe for the same results. But I don't have one. What has changed in me is consciousness itself, or perhaps my awareness of that consciousness.

After witnessing my clients undergo similar metamorphoses, I decided it was time for my second book. Rather than a prescriptive "how-to", you are holding a reminder of what you've always known—that your potentials are unlimited, that the intelligence inside you is the same that governs the rotation of the earth and the paths of the planets, that maybe there's a way to harness that intelligence for what you want in life (instead of what you don't).

If all this talk of planets and spontaneous transformation is sounding a bit woo woo, I'm with you. It took me years of diligent study and practice—the science and engineering of change—to open up to where the intellect and discipline couldn't take me: the mystical, ungraspable magnitude of what we are.

This book dances between science and spirit, practical application and a playful "screw all that" *non-approach*. It's the best I can explain of how the beautiful messiness of life has led me to where I am today. In this mirror of my journey, you'll find concrete, linear representations of how big change can happen, alongside nonlinear explorations of the force that seems to guide and compound all that.

I don't have the arrogance to believe that I can teach you anything. But if you're exhausted by the search and ready to turn within and let your own light lead, then I'm glad you've come here.

It means you're ready to be happy for no reason at all. It means you're ready to embrace new beliefs and drop the ones that were never yours in the first place, to opt out of the noise and live by design, to do what you love and get rich doing it. You're ready to remove layers of untruth to get to the truth, to shine more light on who you really are, to return to play and inherent confidence, and to remember and relax into love.

So, without further ado, get ready to give yourself a whole lot of permission to be YOU.

All Love,

Cortney

CHAPTER 1

Believe

What do you believe in? I mean *really* believe in? What is it that you don't doubt?

If you can uncover your beliefs, you will understand a lot more about the situations, people, and circumstances in your life. You will also begin to see how those same beliefs are drawing specific probability outcomes to you and how you can choose a different belief to attract a different outcome.

For example, you could believe that you can eat whatever you want and not gain a single pound. I know people like this, and it's "true" for them. Alternatively, you could just as easily believe that if you even so much as look at a cake, you get fat, or that drinking green smoothies is the only way to stay healthy and fit. The good (or bad) news is that, whatever you believe, *you're right.*

CAN WE DIRECT OUR BELIEFS?

Right about now, you might be saying, "Hey, Cort, you don't know my situation. I've been struggling with this [*insert the problem here*] my whole life." And let me just say, *I hear you.* Our beliefs become our *identities*, and our identities are very hard to release because they give us a kind of false sense of stability in an ever-changing world.

But here's what I also know: **If we fight for our limitations, we get to keep them.**

So this is an invitation to get curious about your beliefs—the conscious ones and the unconscious ones—and to begin to consider which ones are serving you and which ones are not.

Before we go any further, a quick note about the difference between unconscious and consciously directed beliefs:

What we *unconsciously* believe is what we think is "just the way things are"—a part of our identity (or our world) and something we cannot change. We might be aware of the fact that we hold this belief, but we simultaneously assume that it couldn't be any different. Whether we are aware of these guiding beliefs or not, we can instantly deduce what they are by examining the corresponding results in any particular area of our life.

For example, a client of mine was certain that working fourteen-hour days was the only way to have success on the scale that he desired. When I pointed out that with some simple shifts in his perception and use of time, he would be able to work four-hour days and get far better results, he argued, "It's impossible to work only four hours a day and produce as much as I do, Cort." Since I personally know people who work far less than what I was proposing and produce and earn far more, it was clear that we had to wait on implementing the strategy because his underlying belief that it *had to be hard* wouldn't support the shift. So we had to dismantle the belief first and replace it with a more aligned one. (We'll cover how to do that throughout this book.)

Conscious beliefs, on the other hand, are the ones we actively direct. We know we have agency over these beliefs. For example, someone could start believing that they could become a great musical talent and begin using this belief to shape their behaviors and attitudes, and hence their actions or output. Choosing to *consciously* embrace a new belief can alter the program at an unconscious level, and this shift can take place simultaneously if we hold the new belief unconditionally and with conviction.

UNCONSCIOUS COLLECTIVE BELIEFS THAT SERVE US

Let's go one layer deeper and discuss collective unconscious beliefs that we depend on for more than just identity—the ones we need for survival. These are unquestioned (and largely unexamined) assurances. Some examples: We believe that our hearts will keep pumping blood to our organs and tissues; that our feet, guided by electrical impulses from our brains, will carry on stepping, one in front of another; that the two million working parts of the eye will continue to translate external stimuli and transmit select information to our brains…

When we stop to consider it for a moment, we quickly realize that nearly our entire existence is made possible by that kind of blind belief. We can also call this *unconditional trust* or *faith*.

While we move about our day and decide what to do with our conscious attention, we *trust* that our hearts will keep beating and pumping blood to all our vital organs. We *trust* that the next breath will come after this one. We *trust* that the trillions of biochemical reactions occurring in our body *every second* will continue to conduct business as usual.

If we did not have this basic and fundamental trust or faith, imagine how impossibly complicated life would be.

Every day, about seventy billion cells die in your body; a new intestinal tract appears every three to four days; red blood cells die every three months; the kidney cells renew themselves every year. You are not walking around with the same body you were walking around with a decade ago. Or even *yesterday*. Does it regularly occur to you to examine or even consider any of that? For most of us, the answer is *no*. We will likely go our entire lives being completely unaware of these phenomena, and yet completely dependent upon them. We wouldn't dream of creating a "five-year plan" to make sure it all stays on track, also because our conscious mind simply couldn't cope with such a feat.

So why this incessant attempt to calculate, manipulate, and control certain other aspects of our lives? When we become aware that we are applying this basic underlying faith to more than 99.99999 percent of our day-to-day experience (because we *have to*), we can begin to see how absurd it is that we are not extending this same trust to the less than 0.00001 percent that we decide needs to be "controlled".

My theory is that this attempt at control arises from a fear of surrendering everything to that same Power. It's a destabilizing fact to face that we just don't know, we just *can't* know, what the next moment holds for us. So our conscious awareness tries to set us up in ways that mitigate this vast and limitless unknown. While we might feel we are protecting ourselves in this way, we are also blinding ourselves to the myriad and magnificent creative possibilities available to us in every moment.

HOW DO WE CHANGE OUR BELIEFS TO CREATE MORE POSSIBILITY?

Now, just to be clear: I am not saying that we have absolutely no control over the results in our life. Indeed, we do. It's just not the kind of "make it happen" control that's often dogmatized. Our power of control lies in our ability to *choose where we place our attention*, and this conscious choosing immensely affects our individual and collective reality.

When we place our attention on what we want and align our conscious and unconscious minds to that desire, we become active creators. This alignment cannot be forced. It involves releasing all that is *not* in alignment with the attainment or creation of one's desire and accepting all that *is* in alignment with the mental picture or creative impulse.

You can see how easily this principle applies if you look at the creation of, say, a chair. The carpenter decides to build a chair; she holds the mental image and nothing in opposition to that image (she doesn't think, for example, *What if the chair turns into a couch while I'm assembling the parts?*); then she sets about piecing it together until voilà: we have a chair.

The same creative power applies when our beliefs are in alignment with any other evolutionary impulse we hold. Therefore, our only power of control and the correct use of what we call "free will" rests in *choosing* where and how to direct our *attention*.

Placing your full *attention* on the object of your *intention* is a superpower.

Release the idea of control. Replace it with *choice*. Then use your free will to choose the thoughts and beliefs you will entertain and hold in your consciousness. Direct those thoughts and beliefs to match your creative impulse or intention, and voilà: we have an evolved human being.

TWO WAYS OF EVOLVING (OR TRANSFORMING MATTER)

From personal experience and also from witnessing my clients undergo gradual *and* instantaneous transformations, it is clear to me that we have at least two ways of changing form, or shaping physical matter.

The first takes a step-by-step approach to moving into a new reality for ourselves. I write about this approach in my first book, where I outline the steps to move from wherever you are (your starting point) to where you want to be (your destination, or "future" vision). This approach is a simple and effective way to create something new: If you have a clear understanding of where you are and where you want to be, you can get where you want to go by consistently applying yourself in that direction.

This first method approaches change from a classical physics model of reality, and is characterized by slow and steady steps in the direction of a vision or specific material outcome. Again, this is a very valid and practical approach. The only potential downside is that it is governed by strict rules and takes more time than the second approach.

The second, rapid approach holds the underlying principle and knowing that we are *not* the body and we are *not* the mind, and hence we can alter those expressions in an instant. We still use our conscious intention to decide the new form we wish to take, but this time, we use awareness and attention to rapidly (sometimes instantly) embody that which we've envisioned.

What I'm espousing is not theoretical. In my own life, I have experienced my body change drastically within days; my psyche open up to nonlocality, a connectedness to everyone and everything; and my awareness assume an expansiveness that defies any description.

We can also witness these kinds of phenomena in spontaneous healings, where native healers, like the Kahuna in Hawaii for example, are trained to believe unconditionally in their power to transcend perceived body-mind constraints and perform the so-called miraculous.

My theory and understanding is that these two ways of transforming matter work together. That is, when we consistently apply ourselves in believing and creating something new, there is a point at which *Something Else* joins our efforts to accelerate growth in that direction. Our job is to apply effort and trust, knowing life is working for us and that our vision will fully emerge when we have fully embodied that trust.

It's a bit like the Chinese bamboo, the seed of which is carefully planted and must be tended to for *four years* before it shoots through the soil. When it does emerge from the soil, the Chinese bamboo can grow to *ninety feet in only five weeks*. Likewise, many of the most remarkable human discoveries came on the tail of intense and prolonged concentration and effort (nurturing the seed), *followed by* a kind of relaxed awareness—a relinquishing to something greater, allowing a quantum re-arrangement of consciousness.

I like to think about combining these two approaches as *priming ourselves for God's gifts.** Because, as far as I can tell, *both* deliberate action *and* an almost exasperated or humorous release are required to step into the brilliant vortex of transformation. And here we return again to the power of focused, yet relaxed awareness.

THE FIELD OF ALL POSSIBILITIES

In the study of quantum physics, we are told that a particle is a wave at the same time. It is a wave up until the point of observation (i.e., *attention*). In other words, as soon as we place our attention on the non-physical, it begins to take on physical form. Up until that point, it is simply a probability outcome in an infinite field of probability outcomes.

Translated, this means that *directed attention* holds enormous power.

To me, this also explains why science can find proof of starkly opposing "facts". For example, one study of diet and nutrition will find that carbohydrates are the enemy of a healthy diet and that we should not consume them at any cost, while another study will praise

---

** I use the words God, Force, Source, Light, and Love interchangeably throughout the book. Choose whichever feels right or resonates with you and substitute where needed. See if you can go beyond the concepts the words might represent to you and stay present to whether what's behind them rings true.*

carbohydrates as the ideal energy source for the body. Which is true? What if both studies were simultaneously potentially accurate and simply a result of the scientist finding evidence that confirms a predetermined belief or hypothesis?

YOU FIND WHAT YOU'RE LOOKING FOR (EVERY TIME)

The reality is, we find what we expect to find. Without fail. Every time. And those expectations and consequent "evidence" are a result of what we believe about ourselves and the world around us. Period.

It's as simple (albeit elusive) as that.

To understand a bit more clearly *why* we find what we are looking for we also need to talk about the most sophisticated search engine ever created: your reticular activating system (RAS), which connects the brainstem to the cerebral cortex. The RAS is that part of the brain that is responsible for matching our thoughts, beliefs, and expectations to the environment around us.

The RAS *always* finds what we are expecting to find: the information and circumstances that correspond to our dominant thoughts, questions, and beliefs.

It sorts through extraordinary amounts of data and filters through to our conscious awareness only that which matches our specific search requirements. Since our sensory receptors are exposed to a gargantuan amount of stimuli every day, this fundamental function of the mind is essentially keeping us sane. Without it, we would experience a complete sensory overload and be entirely unable to operate in any conceivably "normal" way.

Unfortunately, however, if not understood and consciously directed, this part of the brain often finds the answers to questions we *don't* want answered. *Why do I always procrastinate? How come I just can't lose the extra weight? What are all the things I don't like about this person/place/situation?* With questions like these, we are misdirecting and misusing this phenomenally powerful tool that is available to all of us.

Again, we are either on autopilot, allowing unconscious beliefs to inform these questions, or we are consciously directing this part of our brain. Which will *you* choose? To be unaware of the questions you're asking, or to ask *way better* questions, like: *What do I enjoy about this person/place/situation? How can I shine brighter? How can I free the way for love?*

The quality of your questions determines the quality of your results in life. So, what version of yourself and others do you wish to find?

TAKING YOUR POWER BACK

The modern mystic and author Neville Goddard talked of the power of belief thus: "We are all born with an infinite power, against which no earthly force is of the slightest significance." Henry Ford put it even more directly with: "Whether you believe it or not, you're right." In other words…

You don't attract what you want. You attract what you *believe* about yourself and the world.

And the questions you're asking (consciously and unconsciously) are a mere reflection of those beliefs and of where you are choosing to place your trust.

When you consciously choose what you want to believe, you are also shaping truth, or reality as you will perceive and experience it. When you hold that decided truth with conviction and ask questions based on that conviction, then reality bends to display that belief. Your actions will also begin to align with that belief and generate the momentum that shapes form or matter (like the chair).

Know that *you can only do what you are*. That is to say, the "doing" happens *through* you as a result of who you *believe* yourself to be. When you have arranged the concept of yourself in a certain pattern (beliefs), your actions will demonstrate that concept in the physical.

This is akin to the phenomenon of magnetism—when particles are arranged in a random, mixed formation there is no magnetic charge, whereas when a number of the same particles face in a single direction, the substance is a magnet. Hence magnetism, just like who you are becoming, is not *created*, but rather *displayed*. The potential exists, as do myriad other probability outcomes, simultaneously.

Now, before we step into the next chapter, THANK YOU for reading this far. What it indicates to me is that you are ready to reclaim your attention and direct it toward beliefs that empower, rather than disempower you. This means that you are in a very small percentage of the world population at the moment of this writing. I congratulate everything it took for you to get here, and I invite you to dive much deeper with me in the chapters that follow.

For now, officially grant yourself permission to *believe*… especially in yourself and in your power to shape a new reality and the most exciting expression of you. And if believing means changing your mind about a lot of stuff, we'll cover how to do that now.

CHAPTER 2

Change Your Mind

What we covered in Chapter 1—reframing and recreating your belief systems—means you have to be willing to change your mind about your current path, if necessary.

The problem is, it can feel straight-up frightening to change your mind about the direction you're heading in, especially if you've been heading in that direction for a long while. Here's the scenario: You're driving one way (current job, business project, life plan) and something inside starts telling you it's the wrong way. Instead of listening and course correcting, you tell yourself you have no choice; you resign yourself to the direction you already chose. Or you risk it all and feel like you're gambling with your life.

But if we take a step back, what we need to decide is not whether or not we should change direction or start anew. What we need to take a close look at is the *instinct* or *nudge* to do so. What is this nudge signaling to us? By questioning the nudge, rather than the direction, we can understand whether or not to entertain or override it, and to what degree.

Here's how you question the nudge: The minute it comes up, you have to give yourself a *timeout*. Take a few moments of stillness to just be with it. Then you get curious and honestly look at whatever emerges in order to determine whether it is there to help or hinder you. You can also use your physical body to test the validity of the nudge (more on that later in this chapter).

Turning inward for the answer like this takes practice, and it runs contrary to the "make it happen" and "just do it" culture we live in, but it's where the gold is. Just to be clear: There's a huge difference between an *expansive* nudge that lets us know it's time to course-correct and a *fear-based* nudge that wants us to change direction on a whim or quit something because it would be easier to give up or because we don't believe that we have what it takes.

I am personally all about keeping commitments, especially when those commitments are derived from a clear vision for ourselves and others. So let me further explain the difference between an *expansive* nudge and a *fear-based* nudge. The first enhances your light; the second diminishes it.

EXPANSIVE NUDGE TO DO OR NOT DO SOMETHING

(listen to the nudge and course-correct)

After only a few weeks of starting to write this book, I kept getting the message that I had a *fiction* story to tell. A story about a woman who lives a glamorous looking life, but who knows she's off track and wants to reinvent herself. I wrote about her for a few mornings and then started to tell myself, "I'm not a fiction writer! I have no idea how to do this! Where is this coming from anyway? I should just concentrate on the non-fiction book I've been writing." And so on…

So I left the fiction to the side and went back to *pushing through* the non-fiction, overcoming my resistance… because that's what we're told we have to do, right? The only problem was that my spirit wasn't in it. *Give Yourself Permission* just wasn't surfacing (maybe because I wasn't giving myself permission? Duh.). I continued to insist until I had to accept (months later) that the fiction book wanted to be written.

So I started writing the fiction book again, and that's when the non-fiction book also got some breathing space and could begin to flow more freely. Simultaneously working on both felt right. It was exciting, and I was back and on track. The nudge was expansive. It wanted me to expand my creativity and trust in myself.

These nudges are gifts from the Universe, a chance to see just how far we can go in exploring the potential available to us in human form.

Have you ever had a nudge like that? Maybe you wanted to write a book or learn an instrument. Maybe you had a nudge *not* to do something because it just didn't feel right, and you couldn't explain it beyond that. I've had those. And whenever I've ignored them, I've paid a heavy price. Again, this kind of nudge is calling us to expand, to grow into more of who we are, which some-times translates to answering a call and other times indicates we need to release or leave behind what is no longer serving us.

FEAR-BASED NUDGE TO DO OR NOT DO SOMETHING

(don't listen to the nudge...go deeper instead)

I don't always want to show up for what I feel called to do. Sitting down every morning to connect with the deepest, truest parts of myself, for example, isn't always easy. Sometimes I want to do *anything else* instead. Sleep in, check my phone, have a snack, make a coffee, order my sock drawer (thank you, Marie Kondo), hop on Netflix... Literally. Anything. Else. When I feel that kind of resistance, I know it's just a series of thoughts trying to distract me from what's most important. And that's when I know I have to return to what's most important.

If you want to live life on your own terms, it's critical to learn to override the short-term satisfaction of distracting yourself from who you want to become.

Since I know how strong that pull can be and because I also know that billions are spent annually to keep us distracted, I take very deliberate steps to master my attention and not give it away so freely. An example of what that looks like in my life: I intentionally start my day with what's most important to me and keep data off on my phone until I have invested at least a couple of hours in what I care about, what pulls my life and vision forward.

Now, I get that it's not easy *at all* to avoid the pings and lights and icons that pop up on our phones. And that's why I don't even expose myself to them until *I decide*. Because too much distraction kills creativity, and those endorphin hits are just too strong to avoid when we overexpose ourselves. But while this kind of nudge (*just check the phone real quick*) is hard to overcome, it's way less insidious than the second kind of fear-based nudge that keeps us from our greatness.

The second way we avoid stepping into our potential is by listening to the inner and outer critics that tell us we shouldn't move forward with our creative and life pursuits because of what other people might think or how they might react to our desire to be more. *Who am I to say/think/do/create/be this [insert whatever it is we got the expansive nudge about]?* This type of nudge can be enormously debilitating because it comes from an innate, primordial need for acceptance and belonging. This kind of fear is primal and sets off alarms in our amygdala—the part of our brain that tells us whether to fly, fight, or freeze.

Where this second kind of fear-based nudge is concerned, I invite you to advance toward your dream, rather than away from it. The cost of not stepping into a fuller potential is astronomical.

One last note about expansive vs. fear-based nudges: You might have noticed how these two types of nudges can work together (or not). If we get an expansive nudge, we can deliberately create fear-based nudges or reminders that highlight the danger of *not* expanding. The more we align these types of nudges, the easier it will be for our psyche to follow in the direction of expansion and evolution.

On the other hand, when these two types of nudges are in opposition to one another, it creates a lot of turmoil in the psyche. One is trying to get us to move in a new, exciting, worthwhile direction, while the other is trying to distract us from doing so. Once we allow ourselves to embrace the excitement and expansion and release the fear and the distraction it breeds, we are upleveling. We are enhancing our life.

Now, you might be saying, "This all sounds great, Cort, but how can I be sure about what kind of nudge it is and if I should listen to it or not?" My answer to that is two-fold:

1. You *do* know. Avoid the "I don't know" story and keep turning inward and listening instead.
2. If for now you sincerely feel like you don't know, there are other ways of sourcing a yes/no response from your body. Let's talk about those…

HOW TO GET STRAIGHT ANSWERS FROM YOUR BODY

Years ago I was attending a course and learning about muscle testing and kinesiology, also referred to as bio-feedback. Most of the attendees were medical professionals of some kind, and I was surprised at how quickly they embraced the techniques being taught. The idea that the body is the ultimate lie detector (and truth teller) resonated with me too, but I wasn't sure about the accuracy of testing the strength of our muscles when confronted with certain statements, beliefs, and decisions.

From what I can remember now, we were taught to keep our gaze looking down and angled at a certain degree (probably to enhance focus while still staying present) and hold an arm out to the side. We had to stay relaxed but also maintain the strength in that arm (try to hold it up) while someone else "tested" true/false statements by pushing down lightly on the outheld arm. If the statement was true, our arm would remain up; if false, the arm would lose strength and go down. For most participants (maybe everyone except for me) there was a noticeable difference in responses to true/false statements.

We explored various ways of using this method, including self-testing in the advanced course, and I was disheartened by not feeling that I could "read" what the muscle was saying. I had a lot of resistance to listening to my body at that time. It was almost like I was disconnected with my physical self and living mostly in my head.

I left the course with this frustration, still feeling so much resistance to the teachings. And that's when I decided to keep going, to move through the fear-based nudge. *I wanted to learn how to listen to my body.* I let go of trying to "figure it out" or control the practice in any way. I also let go of how I was taught to test my muscles. I asked myself: *How does my body want to tell me the truth?* That's when I was met with the answer—or what I call "the sway".

Here's how it works:

1. Ensure you are not distracted during this exercise and that your body is completely relaxed and you don't have any other pressing needs, like hydrating or going to the bathroom.
2. Close your eyes (this runs contrary to how this method is taught, but it works best for me).
3. Ask your body a series of yes/no questions to start to become familiar with how your body sways with true and false statements (for example, "My name is [true test: your name]"; "I live in [false test: different town or city than where you live]").
4. If your body sways forward, that's an indication to go for it or to embrace the statement as true (or at least true for you in this moment).
5. If your body sways backward, it's an indication of falsehood or something being "off" or inaccurate about the statement.
6. Practice and trust that your body will find the perfect way of communicating truth to you.

Testing my body for truth in this way has given me so many "right" answers and powerful experiences that I am often humbled by how accurate the body is in reading a situation or a person or an idea.

YOUR BODY REALLY DOES KNOW

Less than a year after that course, I was working with a client in Stockholm and decided we would try muscle testing for a response to something she was ambiguous about. Even though I was still rocky with it, it just felt right to teach her this technique for getting out of the machinations of the mind and into the simple, direct communication of the body.

I started to test her muscles with the usual "true" phrases:

"I live in Stockholm." (test result: *True*)

"My name is Maja." (test result: *False*)

What?? Maja was the right name! Only two questions in and we weren't getting an accurate reading on her *own name*?

I took one more shot and had her repeat a different name, a man's name:

"My name is Samuel." (test result: *True*)

Okay, now this *really* wasn't working. I mean, here I'd asked her to repeat a male name, one that wasn't even Swedish in origin. Why in the world would her muscle test strong to that?

While I was in my head, cursing myself for trying this kind of thing with an elite corporate executive, I hadn't noticed how ashen her face had become and how she was looking back at me now. "Why did you ask that name?" she inquired with an uncharacteristically soft tone. I sputtered back, "No idea, sorry, maybe this isn't working." At that point she actually started crying. Okay, I thought, why would she be so upset about a failed muscle test?

That's when I got one of the biggest surprises of my career and one of the greatest reminders to trust my instincts and my body. She sputtered out, "That's the name my parents wanted to give me before I was born. They thought I was going to be a boy. They really wanted to have a boy. Me being born a girl was kind of a disappointment. They even 'jokingly' called me by that name for a while after my birth."

To say that I was absolutely blown away would be an understatement. Her body knew. Her body remembered.

Now it was time for her body to release it. (More about how to release what we're holding in our bodies—pain memories, trauma, fears—in subsequent chapters.)

Since I am not an expert at kinesiological testing, I invite you to read *Power vs. Force* by David Hawkins if you want to dive deeper into the science and accuracy of muscle testing. And in the meantime, you can play around with "the sway" or explore other ways your body might have of telling you the truth. When I can't make up my mind or heart about something (usually because

I'm distracted and not fully present with it), I now allow myself to trust this kind of testing and make a decision either way so that I can move forward.

YOUR HEART ALSO KNOWS

Okay, I struggle with platitudes, and "listen to your heart" used to feel like one to me. But clichés are clichés for a reason, and this one holds a potent secret.

The area in your body that corresponds to your heart sends and receives electromagnetic energy and information. It projects signals out into your environment and receives the matching frequency of those signals. According to the Heart Math Institute, your heart's ability to communicate this way is hundreds, if not thousands, of times stronger than that of your cerebral mind. So, an alternative to the sway exercise is tuning into your heart and the area all around your heart.

Normally when we connect our breathing with our heart and focus on one question or circumstance, we will get an immediate answer via physical sensations in this area of the body. If our heart is open to the idea we're giving our attention to, we will feel a sense of expansion and excitement. If instead the feeling we get is one of constriction or tightness, we can immediately take that as a need to course-correct or shift our focus.

Keep in mind that we have several "body minds" (or energy centers). These centers correspond to the physical organs in our body and also contain untold amounts of energy and data. So, in the same way, you can tune into another center—your gut, for example—where you will have, yet again, another "truth detector" in the sensations you feel there regarding any particular decision, person, event, or idea.

Take a moment now and consider where your most accurate readings come from. Do you often say things like, "My gut tells me" or "My heart's just not in it"? That's a clue to where you naturally and spontaneously source answers for yourself. And the more you tune into it, the stronger this truth-teller will become.

WHEN WE GET AN *INACCURATE* READING

Sometimes we can have that sense of expansion or constriction and attribute it to the wrong catalyst. All this means is that our attention is fragmented and our body is picking up on the fact that something is off, which may or may not be what's right in front of us. If we're unsure about the "reading", it's a good idea to eliminate any other distraction for the time it takes to focus as clearly as possible on exactly what we want to test so that we can get an accurate body response.

Another time our instincts can be off is when we are judging or criticizing a person or situation. For most of us, freeing ourselves from judgment is a lifelong pursuit. Remembering times when our thoughts were wrong about someone or something can help us reset to get a more accurate picture that then allows us to tap into our body wisdom.

A time when judgment got in my way was back when I was working in corporate and heading up an industry-wide group. I was working on a big project with this one guy, who I'll call Alex, when he suddenly became despondent. He was ignoring my calls and his delayed responses to my emails seemed short and annoyed. I started to wonder what I'd done. *Why did he dislike me?* Yep, it's embarrassing to admit, but I made it all about me. Exchanges like this continued for weeks until, thank goodness, I conjured the courage to just ask what *he* was feeling: "Hey, Alex, what's going on? We used to have a great working relationship. Did I do something to offend or annoy you?"

I wish I had asked those questions sooner. His response was, "Cort, I'm sorry. Two months ago, I found out I have cancer. Everything else just doesn't really seem to matter anymore." Whoa. To say I felt like a self-centered fool is an understatement. Here I'd been, annoyed about his dismissive behavior, while all along he'd been fighting a serious battle. Alex reminded me that day that we have *no* idea what's happening in someone else's world. I wish my inner dialogue had been quieter at that time in my life. Maybe I would have accurately read his despondency and talked to him sooner.

The point: At times, we can misread people's motives, and if we're projecting our own issues onto others, we've missed the boat. So my best advice is to always assume the absolute best about people and get real quiet before testing any feelings to the contrary. The clarity that emerges will make a change of mind a lot easier.

The last bit I'll say about changing our minds (and using our body to help us do that) is this:

I've seen so many people stay in jobs or relationships or compromising circumstances just because they were too afraid of the unknown to follow the instinctual nudge to change, too afraid to ask more empowering questions that would lead to a shift in perception, too afraid of how others would respond to the change.

Opportunity is generous, though, and it keeps knocking. The choice is yours: stay comfortably *uncomfortable*—likely leading to a downward trajectory—or trust that you *can* create a new reality for yourself—and soar upward. Thus, changing your mind is about aligning yourself with who you really are and trusting that evolutionary instinct.

So, before we go any further together, know that it's okay to change your mind…about people, situations, your past, your future, and—most important of all—about who you are and who you can be *now*. Because your inner self never had to change its mind; it always knew. And it's what will guide you to what we're about to cover—*doing what you love*.

CHAPTER 3

Do What You Love

Once you've worked up the courage to change your mind, you can also start giving yourself permission to do more of what you love and less of what you don't. Doing what you love means waking up (most days) with a feeling of gratitude and excitement about the stretch of time right in front of you.

Doing what you love is about consciously deciding to shine your light through your work.

Too many people are doing what they *don't* love, viewing their work as a means to an end. *"Once I finish this, I'll finally be able to [fill in the blank with what they actually enjoy doing]."* That kind of reverse order thinking results in a rather unhappy and unhealthy world.

It's heartbreaking that we live in a society that says so few of us can find, much less *do*, what we love and earn a living that way. This is simply an untruth. We all come into physical form with innate proclivities and abilities. We all have very specific drives and dreams *for a reason*. And we can discover more of these as we grow into each one.

Even if we're afraid that we can't make lots of cash doing what we love (which we *can*—more about that in the next chapter), what sense does life make if we spend the majority of it in a role that wasn't designed for us, in a job or career that doesn't fulfill us, in a Thank-God-It's-Friday weekly loop? What if instead we could "Thank God It's *Now*"? What if every day we could hop out of bed excited to step into another glorious twelve- to sixteen-hour unfolding of who we are becoming? What if instead of "making a living" we were *being a living*…a living expression of what's most beautiful and noble in us? What would life look like then?

It's the ultimate act of trust and faith to believe that we can do what we love. It requires us to take steps in that direction and *persist*, even (especially) when external circumstances don't immediately align to our desires and dreams.

How do we persist? Here are a few keys I've discovered over the years.

KEY #1: PLAN LESS, FEEL MORE

I used to have a plan for everything. A tidy, little outline to fit my work (and my world) into. And it was all stuff I *had* to do. Not what I *wanted* to do. Not what I loved. Then, back in 2017, I decided to go for my dreams. I chose to scrap what I'd been taught in the world of business (Excel files and strategy docs and five-year Power-Points) and grabbed a cardboard box instead. I cut out a square a little bigger than my head and drew twelve boxes to represent the twelve months of that year.

Then I took fluorescent paint markers (I'm serious) and proceeded to put huge dreams in every box. Dreams it "should have" taken way more time, by traditional planning standards, to bring to life. One box held "publishing my first book"; another one boldly announced my first TEDx Talk; another said I would spend an entire month in the US (something I hadn't been able to do for over a decade because of work demands). I had *zero* idea how to do any of that. It was just a dream. Lots of dreams.

What happened that year was nothing short of magical and gave me the first insight into the power of simplified, *unforced* focus.

Every Single Dream on that piece of cardboard came to life. Clarity and trust were the *only* essential ingredients.

These days I don't even have a plan to make a plan. I just get real clear on the next beautiful dream, and then I allow myself to experience it *now*—to see it represented in some way and then to *feel into* the sensations it provokes in my body and psyche. This inner experiencing (in anticipation of the outer experiencing) gives me the confidence that there's nothing that separates me from the creation of my dream because I can *already feel it*. And that inner alignment allows my behaviors and actions, as well as the circumstances and events around me, to start to match the frequency or energy of the dream itself, thus calling it into physical form or reality.

Exercise: Create your own "non-plan"

Step 1 – Consider how you learn best, or what *imprints* on you most easily. Which of your senses is most receptive to new learning? Is it your sense of smell or taste that leaves a lasting imprint? Or are you more influenced by visual, auditory, or touch cues? It could be that you learn best through a combination of these senses or in some other way that is unique to you. Once you've pinpointed what works best for you, you're ready for the next step.

Step 2 – Are there any desires or dreams you've had for a while? (Prolonged desire usually indicates an evolutionary impulse, as opposed to a whim that quickly changes.) What kind of experiences would you most desire to live? What external or sensorial representation of this dream would you enjoy creating? Examples could be a picture board or an audio recording or time spent envisioning the experience while smelling your favorite essential oil. Or maybe a simple cardboard calendar, like the one I created. How can you claim or otherwise represent this expression in the simplest way possible?

However you choose to connect your senses to your present-future dream, remember to *play*. Give yourself permission to not have it all figured out, as you keep in mind that being *you* and expressing your gifts is meant to be fun.

KEY #2: LET YOURSELF BE SURPRISED

With your "non-plan" in hand, another gift will begin to emerge: the delight of being surprised.

Do you remember when you were a kid and you went to sleep with your imagination bubbling with excitement at the prospect of what was awaiting you the next day? Do you remember waking up like that? Maybe on a day when your class had a field trip or when you expected to see your crush at the library after school? You just knew something unpredictable and exciting was awaiting you…

Most of us are so entrenched in our daily routines that we forget to leave space for the unplanned, unforeseen gifts that are around us everywhere. It's as if we intentionally limit or avoid the unexpected so we won't be rocked out of our so-called comfort zone. We stick to the stories of who we believe ourselves to be, and we lose contact with the mystery of the moment. *We choose predictability over play and wonder.*

This happens so gradually and unnoticeably as we grow that we forget what it was like to *not* be overidentified with specific ideas of who we are or what is possible for us. We forget what it's like to morph into different expressions that allow us to play and discover new roles or potentials.

One way I've found to tap into fresh, new parts of me that want to be expressed is to switch things up long enough to see that it doesn't have to be a certain way… that there's no preordained script that we have to follow in life.

There are many ways to shake it up so more surprise and delight are available to us.

Years ago, for example, I decided to learn to use my non-dominant hand to write and do everything else I normally did only with my dominant hand—like cooking, brushing my teeth, and navigating with a mouse. At first, the tendency to use my dominant hand was so strong that it felt like a gargantuan (and potentially useless) effort to relearn.

As I persisted, however, I gradually came to realize that this new practice was taking me out of what was *familiar* and into a kind of presence that is required when we don't yet know how to do something, when we don't think we know the best way, or that it's the *only* way. It's when we agree with ourselves to start from scratch and see what happens.

When we're curious like this, we start to open ourselves up to new experiences and the chance to learn more about what we love and enjoy doing.

Exercise: Get curious and switch it up

Step 1 – Is there something you could play around with doing differently? Maybe it's just taking a different route on your drive to work, or leaving fifteen minutes early to sit in a coffee shop with a journal and a pen to write about what you love to do (see the last key in this chapter).

Step 2 – Start noticing moments of your day that were exciting, unexpected, and novel. Take a few moments, even now, to close your eyes and reflect on your day or week: *What events or circumstances or people excited you or left you with a happy, grateful feeling?*

The more you practice *playing* and *noticing* like this, the more you will open up to the magic and mystery of your own evolution, as you shed layer after layer of who you thought you *had* to be so that you can grow into all that you *can* be.

KEY #3: TAP INTO THOSE ACTIVITIES THAT LIGHT YOU UP

In order to start doing more of what we love, we have to *know* what we love. Seems obvious, but many times we lose touch with what we love as we bury it under pressures and carefully crafted illusions of what we think we should be doing instead.

What you love is a spark that can turn everything on for you. If you're actively listening to yourself (see my first book, *Change Starts Within You*), then you will start to feel this spark. Some people feel it in their heart, some in their gut. You might feel it somewhere else, like an activation at the base of your spine. Regardless of where you feel it, it will likely feel pleasurable. Or it might be slightly uncomfortable, like a steady burning impulse that is pushing you to action.

This is the truth that lives in your body and serves as a guidance system to help you make the next accurate choice. Here's one story of what that might look and feel like, and what happens when we listen to it:

A few years back, a client of mine was considering changing her business model. She had a multiple six-figure online empire and wanted to transition into doing most of her work offline. Her dreams were to write a book, start speaking on stage, and do 1:1 high-level mentoring on the side. She'd grown tired of being online all the time and craved more direct (rather than virtual) relationships with her audiences and clients. But *obviously*, she was frightened of leaving such a lucrative online business and didn't have the slightest idea where to start.

So she kept at her online work, becoming increasingly more irritable and frustrated as she stayed in the fear of not believing she could leave it or that she had it in her to create something new. The pain of not listening to her gut (that's where the physical sensation of discomfort was for her) became so great that she developed inflammation and weight gain all around that area of her body.

She was at her limit, and that was when she found my first book and reached out, instinctively guided again to something that reflected her dreams back to her and could open her up to giving herself permission to *change her mind*, to *believe* it was possible for her.

Our inner guidance is like that. It's steering us in the direction that will help us arrive not only where we need to be, but also in the fastest way possible. When we're fighting this inner guidance, we usually feel exhausted and worn out. When we ignore it, we typically feel confused, apathetic, or aimless.

When instead we listen to this inner guidance, a lot of things that would seem hard to others become almost effortless to us.

Luckily, she ultimately chose to follow that guidance and embark on a whole new adventure, and today she is making even more money (see next chapter) doing what she really wants to be doing—what she loves.

In case you're wondering, this transition didn't happen overnight. It was the result of her understanding what she truly cares about and then prioritizing and finding ways to express that in her life.

Here are a couple of exercises to help you start doing the same.

Exercise #1: What do you love?

Take a clean sheet of paper and pen and begin to reflect on what you love. What lights you up? How would you spend more or most of your time if you *could*? If no one—*including yourself*—was telling you what to do, how would you be living your life?

Go ahead, write your list. Here's mine, if it helps:

What I love: Visiting new places. Easy, comfortable travel. Meeting new, awesome people. Giving and preparing talks. Sharing new ideas, sharing old ideas. Making lifetime connections. Dress-up parties. Dancing. Opening my heart to someone and something new. The water, and floating and moving through it. What it feels like when I come out of a super cold lake or sea or ocean. Small, local, cool coffee shops where I can work and dream and write songs. Learning. The moment when something you *thought* becomes something you *know*. Fresh flowers and plant life. Soft grass under an even softer blanket. Guitar sing-along picnics. Riding my bike to this little unknown "beach" on the river. I absolutely adore the sea and the sun and the moon. Eating healthy, happy food and really tasting and enjoying it. Mocktails or a glass of wine as the sun is setting or as I'm cooking up a yummy dinner. I love, love, love laughing, and I love people who make me laugh. Movies that inspire me to believe in the best kind of "impossible" and remind me of beauty and love and the power of will and belief. Watching or feeling the light turn on in someone, and being part of that or a catalyst for it. I love beauty, and I love noticing beauty in others or in nature. Talking for hours with my friends. Reading, especially romantic-thrilling fiction. I love that I can speak more languages than the one I was born into. Going on adventures that stretch me into new, upgraded versions of me. Receiving body and mind treatments. Making the choices that match my highest vision of myself. I love, love, love when I can feel the light in me shining super bright.

Exercise #2: What are the important, not urgent things you've been putting off?

Grab another clean sheet of paper and reflect on things that are important to you, that you know you want to be doing, but that don't seem urgent, or that you don't prioritize for some other reason. This list might include exercising, getting out in nature, calling your close friends for a catch-up, telling someone how grateful you are to have them in your life, finally asking someone out who you like.

Consider this when creating your list: *If you died tomorrow, what would you be sorry you hadn't done or experienced yet?*

When I first did an exercise like this, I realized I wanted to tell all of my brothers and sisters how much they mean to me and all the things that are so cool about each of them. The very next day, I started calling them. I told them what I appreciate about them, how much I love them, and that the world would be a worse place without 'em.

That was a long time ago, and I'm not even sure now if any of them remember me calling like that. But I remember. And I feel better for having done it.

You might be wondering, of all the things you might do to uncover what you care about, why this exercise? Here's why:

Most of us spend our days distracting ourselves with the constant drip or information, or putting out fake fires, or just generally prioritizing other people's agendas and interests. **When we stop instead to reflect on what *really matters*, we begin to consciously direct our life and create events that mean something.**

This second exercise is so revelatory that if you spend time with it every month or two, you will start to flip your entire relationship with time and the world around you. You will wake up more often with a smile on your lips, laughter ready, eyes sparkling. And you'll also begin to understand the *inherent value* in doing what you love, and how that inner sense of value translates into external abundance of all kinds—a wealth that nothing and no one can ever take away from you.

Let's talk about that kind of wealth now.

Make a Lot of Money

Alright, so you're giving yourself permission to do more of what you love. Excellent. Now it's time to invite in the abundance that comes with that.

One of the primary reasons people—especially women—do not give themselves permission to make a lot of money is that there are some unspoken, collective ideas about money that really don't serve us. Unconscious systemic beliefs that keep us from seeing our true value include: the belief that anyone else can do what we do (and maybe better); that our core talents are only something we do for "fun", not something that can earn us a living; that we don't deserve to make a lot of money; or that making a lot of money might alienate us from friends and family. This is just a tiny sampling of the kinds of beliefs that consciously or unconsciously hold us back from that currency, or flow, that we call money.

The good news is that you don't have to be aware of all the conditioning that has resulted in your current money situation. All you need is to begin to be aware of, understand, and embrace some basic principles related to wealth accumulation.

PRINCIPLE #1: WEALTH IS AN INSIDE JOB

I'm going to tell you a secret that took me a *very* long time to uncover: the greatest riches you will ever know are *inside* you. This isn't a platitude. It's the ultimate truth about wealth. If you focus on cultivating wealth inside you—a wealth of gratitude, of love, of peace—there will be no end to the external riches that match that intention.

As counterintuitive as it may seem in a society that tells us to "hustle" and "make it happen", your main job is to connect with the *all-sufficiency within you.*

The more you commit to releasing external attachments and letting that inner wealth lead, the richer you will become.

PRINCIPLE #2: MONEY IS AN OUT-PICTURING OF YOUR BELIEFS

Money is simply an out-picturing of the beliefs you've held up until now, especially your beliefs about love and your sense of deservedness.

Again, it took me ages to make this connection. Up until realizing this truth, I held the very disempowering belief that *there wasn't enough for me.* That belief came from the numbers game of growing up in a family of five children. Understanding the origin was helpful, but what shifted things for me was dedicating myself to a new belief—the belief that there is an abundance of riches, material and ethereal, available to me always, when I acknowledge the wealth *within* me.

What new belief do *you* want to dedicate yourself to? You get to set a new one at any moment. It's time.

PRINCIPLE #3: NO ONE ELSE CAN DO YOU

You are the only human on the planet (1 in *8 billion*) who has your combination of talents, experience, stories, flaws, passions, and gifts. In other words, you are an irreplaceable piece of a masterpiece puzzle. No other piece can take your place, and the puzzle is incomplete without your contribution.

How valuable is *invaluable*?

Last time I checked, a resource that is necessary and that is *extremely* rare is worth inestimable amounts. (And a puzzle that's missing one piece is like a punch in the eye. We'll search *everywhere* for that piece.)

This is the truth about your value. You are the most precious commodity in the world. The gifts you specifically are here to offer are irreplaceable and yours alone. They are what you must bring forth in order to prosper.

PRINCIPLE #4: WHERE LOVE IS, MONEY IS

Maybe you love to make people laugh. I know people who make millions with this talent.

Maybe you tell stories that keep people mesmerized. Again, those who can do this can easily attract great wealth.

What do you love to do? What turns on your inner light?

If you love it, many other people will love it. And where love is, money is. Which means you can get very wealthy serving those who want or need your talent or interest, especially as you continue to develop and hone it. Maybe it's not your ultimate talent, but it can lead you to the next one and the next one. A delightful journey into who you're *allowing* yourself to become…

PRINCIPLE #5: GRATITUDE IS THE MASTER KEY TO WEALTH

When asked the secret of wealth, Sir John Templeton, one of the greatest investors of all time, responded with one word: *Gratitude.*

Prosperity consciousness is based in a felt sense of gratitude. When you invite the *physical sensations* of gratitude into your body, you are sending an electromagnetic signal that calls more reasons to be grateful (or reflections of that consciousness) back to you.

Take a moment and write one page of everything you're grateful for. Do this every day for a month and you will start to see what you might call "miracles" but what are really the natural result of you placing your attention on the love and beauty and richness that is ever present within and all around you.

Now that you have knowledge of these principles, you'll want to deepen your understanding by consistently placing your attention on them until you start to see evidence of them in your life. The most powerful way to do this is to "wash your brain" with them every morning and every night.

One of the things I frequently say on stage is, "You're either 'brainwashing' yourself with clean water or with dirty water. It's your choice." We're brainwashing ourselves all the time anyway (see: "collective unconscious/ default beliefs" covered in Chapter 1) so we might as well be doing it with the clean stuff. The principles above are examples of *clear knowing*, and the more you repeat them to yourself and integrate them into your under- standing of life, the more you will experience enhanced states of inner and outer wealth.

A few other things to keep in mind as you shift your per- spective about making money doing what you love:

1. **It's never too late.**

    Many of us spend a lot of time and energy com- plaining (or brainwashing ourselves) that we should have started something sooner. When we take that same energy and direct it to start- ing now, we're perfectly on time. Did you know that Morgan Freeman started his acting career at the age of fifty? Before that, he was a U.S. Air Force veteran and worked as a mechanic; he also worked as a driver and an announcer for a local radio station. I didn't know all that before writing this book. But I did know that Morgan Freeman is an Academy Award winning actor and one of the highest paid performers in Hollywood. The point: It's never too late to give your gifts the space they need to create all the joy of abundance that they are meant to create in your life.

2. **Brainwashing is most effective first thing in the morning and last thing at night.**

   Your brain is most programmable or receptive to new ideas upon waking and right before you nod off. The reason for this is that you are entering into or coming out of brainwave frequencies—alpha, theta, delta (more on those in the next chapter)—that are conducive to new pattern recognition and imprinting. So you'll want to capitalize on these times of day to set yourself up for this new wealth consciousness. All you have to do is focus on the principles for a few minutes shortly after waking and/or right before bed.

3. **It's okay if you're not totally sure what you love to do or if others make fun of you.**

   Look at what people say about you—your talents and natural gifts—and how those might be useful in this world. Start small and don't be afraid if someone diminishes or makes fun of your talent or gift. When I was growing up, my teachers would often remark that I was a "natural born teacher." I didn't identify with this or even understand what they meant, but I did know that I loved to help other kids understand stuff, to simplify things and tell stories in a way that I felt made more sense of what we were learning. In a very non-linear way, this led to what I do today. It wasn't always easy to believe I could turn it into a lucrative career, and on occasion I received some fairly harsh dissuasion from others, but I kept at it. And I'm super happy I did.

4. *Never exchange your time for money.*

Replace your hourly rate with a "results" rate. What kinds of results do you create for people? When others talk of how you've helped them, what do they say? The more you focus on getting really great at what you love and using that gift for the benefit of others, the more you will discover the truth of the second principle: your total irreplaceability and how you are meant to contribute to the bigger picture (or puzzle). Your time here is something you will never get back. Your gifts, when shared with others, are immortal. Focus on your gifts, not your time.

5. You can only *do* what you *are.*

The "doing" is being done through you—it is the result of who you believe yourself to be. It was the great motivational orator Les Brown who said, "In order to do what you've never done, you have to become who you've never been." I love that reminder of embodying the desired state or essence of what you want to see in your life and letting that guide your actions. So focus on *being* the kind of person who does what needs to be done to live into your vision.

START BELIEVING IN *YOU*

Okay, let's see how these principles and insights play out in the real world.

Let's take another look at that client we saw in Chapter 3, the one who had a lucrative online business but was feeling called to let that go so she could focus on an idea she loved a lot more—writing books and giving talks.

She had no prior experience writing or giving lectures. But, just like Morgan Freeman (or anyone else), she had to start somewhere. She began by creating a list of "talk titles" of subjects she was qualified to speak on. For example: "How to create a super profitable online business" or "Expert advice for creating an online course." Then, she started to look at conferences and events that were focused on similar topics. From there, she drafted an introductory email and a one-page speaker sheet that she began sending to the main organizers of these events and to select speaker agents to represent her.

On the writing side, she was inspired to present the mindset—and heartset—needed to create a successful business. So she began by listing out what understandings and practices had really helped her create her business, and then considered what ideas could be hooks for her book and how she could develop those hooks into chapters. Then, she began the most important part of writing any book: *she wrote*. She wrote every morning for a couple of hours until things started to take shape.

Now, there are many other actions she took for both of these projects, but the really important thing to note is that she was *becoming* the kind of person who takes those kinds of actions. She was believing in her vision. She was feeling into the dream. She *already was* the speaker, the writer.

And in order to do that, she had to give up fears about it being too late, or her not being good enough. She had to go through the discomfort (and sometimes pain) of starting over, of growing into someone new. She had to begin brainwashing herself with the notion that she was already the person she desired to be.

In this reinvention process, she had to keep focusing on what she loves, what she wants to share with the world. She had to trust that her ideas and ways of presenting them were hers alone, that no one else could tell that story from her perspective. And every day she conjured up the gratitude and *inner wealth* awareness to keep her going.

"If you bring forth what is within you, what you bring forth will save you. If you do not bring forth what is within you, what you do not bring forth will destroy you."
– Gospel of Thomas, verse 70

THE LIGHT THAT IS MEANT TO SHINE THROUGH YOUR FORM

In my own experience working with the principles I'm sharing with you in this chapter, I have encountered the most awe-inspiring events and material and ethereal abundance—everything from significant client retainers with companies like Universal Music Group to invitations to speak at the most impressive gatherings, like a recent leadership event on Necker Island.

One such example that I'd like to share is from a talk earlier this year in Bogotá, Colombia. I was invited to give a keynote address for Tatiana Arias—one of the most brilliant women I know—at her global event RED, with an audience of over a thousand entrepreneurial women. The production quality of this event was the best I'd ever seen (which is really saying something since I go to a lot of conferences). It was hard to not be distracted by the lights, the massive stage, and the brilliance of all the women in attendance.

With all of that external stimulation, it normally would have been hard for me to keep my focus centered in the truth of why I was there—to remind all those beautiful women of the power they hold inside. That each one of them is an essential piece of the puzzle. And that it is time to bring their gifts forward with the confidence they deserve to embody.

As Tatiana was introducing me and sharing my list of achievements and experience with the crowd, I was backstage praying for God—that Force/Source energy—to use me. I was determined to allow my ego on stage *only* as a supporting actor to the light that is meant to shine through my form (and every form). To stay centered in this truth, I used the power of my mind to block out all the old conditioning of needing to prove or demonstrate anything and relaxed into the knowing that we are all "It".

"There is a force in the universe, which, if we permit it, will flow through us and create miraculous results."
– Mahatma Gandhi

If you knew the love that is available to you in every moment, it would bring you to your knees. It has brought me to my knees many times. The event in Colombia was one of those times. Afterward, I went into ecstatic states of consciousness, not because of the external feedback (which was also ecstatic—two hours of Q&A and four standing ovations), but because that source energy was still pulsating through my being, still informing the environment within and all around me.

This is one of those experiences that I am hesitant to talk about because words are inadequate to describe what happens to and through us when we are centered in love and committed to that inner light (much more on this in Chapter 10), but I needed to share this story with you. Because, my guess is that, if you're holding or listening to this book and you've made it this far, a big part of you knows that you are inherently worthy of your dreams. That you don't want to, and *don't have to,* accept the unconscious systemic beliefs that may still be active in certain areas of your life. That you are ready for the light within to shine bright without. That you're ready to be free. That you're ready to make wealth mean much more than just money.

So, it's time to open up to that infinite abundance. To hold tight to what and who you love with the tenacity of a mama bear. It's gonna be a wild ride. But I promise it'll be super FUN.

CHAPTER 5

Have Fun, Play!

When we're doing what we love (letting that light shine through us) and reaping the rewards (material and ethereal), we naturally start having a lot more fun. And when we're having fun, we feel more "in love" and reap even greater rewards. It's a virtuous cycle.

In my work advising some of the world's leading corporations and universities, I've consistently found that the most enthusiastic and successful teams are the ones laughing in and out of the conference rooms and finding ways to enjoy themselves. Instead of working *hard*, they work *smart*, capitalizing on one another's talents and interests (see previous chapter).

This isn't to say that these teams don't put in a lioness's share of work, because they do, but it doesn't really feel like "work" when you love it and you're having fun.

Same goes for the profession or vocation of your choosing. If you're doing what you love, it will feel like a game.

———

What does fun look like for you? Not that long ago, I had no idea how to answer that question. I mean, I know there were times when I was having fun. But how to *be* fun was unclear.

When we're "being fun" the people and circumstances that match that frequency come on over to meet us. So the intention is really to *live fun* or *be fun*. This means finding the laughter within, the openness and fluidity within.

And that's what happens when we're enjoying ourselves. We let that open fluidity lead. We let go of what it looks like, what people might say about it. We stop looking to anyone else but our own self for confirmation or approval. We relax, allowing our mind and body to stay fresh and inspired, which literally alters our chemical makeup.

THE CHEMICAL—AND *ALCHEMICAL*—MAGIC OF FUN

Having fun is like drinking a chemical/alchemical cocktail that reduces stress and increases happiness. Enjoying ourselves makes us more creative and innovative, sparking new ideas and solutions to problems. If we could take a live mind-body video of what's happening when we're having fun, here's what we'd see:

- The release of the neurotransmitter **dopamine**, often referred to as the "feel good" hormone, associated with pleasure, motivation, and reward. When we're experiencing something pleasurable or having fun, dopamine is jazzing it up even more. Dopamine can also help regulate mood and motivation and enhance memory and focused learning.

- The secretion of the neurotransmitter **serotonin**, which is responsible for mood regulation and feelings of well-being. Serotonin is released when we experience positive emotions, such as joy, happiness, and fun. Among its many benefits, it also helps reduce symptoms of depression, regulate appetite, and improve the quality of our sleep.

- The hormone **oxytocin** is also joining the party. Commonly referred to as the "cuddle hormone" and associated with social bonding and trust, this hormone is generally released when we're having fun with others. Oxytocin can also help decrease stress and anxiety, improve sexual function, and regulate metabolism.

- We'd also see a healthy dose of **endorphins**. These "feel good" chemicals are naturally produced by the body and act as painkillers, increasing our resilience to stress and decreasing our perception of fatigue. Endorphins also help improve mood and boost energy levels.
- The hormone and neurotransmitter **adrenaline** is also released when we're having fun. Adrenaline increases our alertness and boosts our energy and immune system. It also increases focus, improves physical performance and endurance, and helps with digestion and metabolism.

All that from just having fun. So why not?

PARTY'S OVER: COMMON PARTY KILLERS

Let's look at some of the reasons why we don't give ourselves permission to have fun, or the ways we get in our own way:

1. **Taking ourselves too seriously.**

    Yikes, I've totally been guilty of this one in the past. When we forget that life is supposed to be fun, it's really hard for that light we were talking about in the last chapter to run its magic through us. Being serious has become such a socially acceptable form of so-called "realism" or "professionalism" that we can easily fall prey to it, creating a rigidity in mind and body that blocks the flow of our dreams and creativity. We must break free of this. The best way I've found: laughter. (More on this in a sec.)

2. **Believing it has to be hard.**

    We're so conditioned into believing that we have to "make it happen" and "strive for perfection" and "work, work, work" that when something comes easy, we discredit it or discount it as "luck". I used to wear a big blue T-shirt that read, *"Nothing worth doing is ever easy."* I wore this thing all the time—not because of its message, but because of its comfort. Until one day, I asked myself, "Why? Is this even true? Is it what I want to believe?" The answer came: This doesn't have to be *my* truth. The truth I embrace now is that the closer we get to our true nature, the easier it becomes to embody it in all our outward expressions, turning work into play. (I threw away the shirt, btw.)

3. **Caring too much about what other people think.**

    This is a super hard habit to break for most of us because it is linked to one of our most primordial needs: acceptance. But when we care too much about the opinions (good and bad) of others, we are blocking fun and flow in our lives. In order to step into more joyful and expanded versions of ourselves, we've got to be willing to release our fears around how other people will judge or label us. Or as my sister Stacey beautifully puts it, "What other people think of you is none of your business." (Paradoxically, it is the people who care the least about what others think who ultimately receive the most approval.)

4. **Worrying about stuff we have no control over.**

   Bob Marley once said something along the lines of, "Worrying is like praying to the devil." Every time we worry, we are drawing that probability outcome to us. We are calling in the very thing we want to avoid. We are lost in the illusion of needing to control the 0.0001 percent (see Chapter 1) that, in truth, we have *no* control over. Again, we are so conditioned into believing that worry is a good and 'natural' thing that we have forgotten that worry enforces the very thing we wish to heal in ourselves and others. Focusing instead on what we want—and what we *love*—is the fastest way back to fun.

So, now that we've glanced at the main ways we block fun and flow, let's look at some quick, but powerful remedies.

KEEP THE PARTY GOING: RESET BUTTONS

Yawning and laughter are two of the simplest ways to reset your nervous system and take your body out of the fight-flight-freeze state or stress response. The key is to not overthink it and just go to the first instinctive relaxation response to help get you back into party mode.

Yawning: The best kept secret of neuroscience

Yawning—sometimes referred to as "the best kept secret of neuroscience—is a natural breathing "technique" that improves your overall health and ability to cope with stressful situations. It energizes and relaxes you at the same time. It helps with sleep, mood, and anxiety, and it discharges tension and fatigue. Elite athletes use yawning to prepare for and unwind after critical competitions or events. Animals use it before and after a hunt. Yawning has another fabulous side effect of bonding us to others (because it releases oxytocin), so yawn with your family and friends whenever you can. In general, let this be your go-to "meditation" whenever you feel triggered or stuck and want to open to fun.

Laughing: The miracle drug

I once gave a workshop in L.A. and asked participants to sit in a circle with me and laugh hysterically. I awkwardly started us out by opening my mouth and laughing out loud. Everyone clumsily joined in with me, embarrassed at first. In less than a minute, our "mirror neurons" were activated and we were all *truly* laughing. Hysterical, joyful laughter. After a couple of minutes like that, we all felt lighter than sparrows. We couldn't stop smiling, the lines on our faces were visibly reduced, and the sparkle in our eyes was brighter. I consider laughter to be one of the highest forms of "meditation"—or becoming fully present with the moment.

WHEN WE OPEN UP TO RELAXED PLAY

Now, you might be wondering why all this talk about cultivating an attitude of fun and play and how that mixes with discipline and what can sometimes feel like despair in the incremental day-to-day effort of creating a life you love. Let me explain.

All of the breakthroughs I've had in my business and life have come *after* trying to "figure it out". That original effort was critical, but it was only when I got playful and stopped clinging to the limits of the intellect that the realization or insight I needed became apparent. I had to release all the seriousness and stubborn effort and open up to relaxed curiosity and a kind of goofiness…

———

Five or six years ago, I was in the south of England with my friend Elisabet. We had been intensely studying principles of neuroscience and varying states of consciousness, determined to alter our own, to see if we could reach awakened states of theta, delta, maybe even gamma brainwave frequencies (more on these in the next chapter). We spent numerous hours in diligent meditation and tried every which way to "get in" through focused effort. Elisabet had some breakthroughs, but I didn't.

By the end of the week, I went off on my own to sulk in front of the English Channel. I was exasperated. I thought, *what's wrong with me? How come I can't have a breakthrough? Whatever, I give up.* I relaxed. With every sigh, I let the tension of *trying* to generate a specific outcome leave my body. I let go of the expectation. And then something super funny happened: I got goofy. I decided that my despair was rather funny. I laughed and released even more tension, more rigidity.

BOOM.

Next thing I knew, I was transported into states that I can only call *Satori*, or spontaneous awakening.

That is a big statement, so I will let the following writings that came through me shortly after the experience, speak for me here. If you will read these "writings from beyond" with that same playful curiosity and willingness to let go of figuring it out, maybe the insights will open your heart to this ecstasy within.

Writings From "Beyond"

I was fully there and yet not there at all.
Some "thing" began to take over my body.
I could no longer control any of what I'd worked so
carefully to control for so many years.

I began to write in a way I'd never written before.

And then, what came through next was:
"This is how you really write."
And I began to laugh and weep because that is what
my daughter Gaia had told me years before, that I was
writing in the wrong way. "This is how you really write,"
she had said to me.
She knew.
And then I asked, "Do I write with my right or my left?"
And the answer came: "Both."
And then I let go of more control.
I didn't care how it looked.
I couldn't.
For once, I couldn't.
And then: "Do you see now that it never mattered?"
And then: "It's time for you to see who you really are."

The last word I wrote is almost entirely
illegible but it says:
GOD.

There was much weeping and unbridled
laughter and a complete lack of body control, and
a few times I wondered if I'd be stuck that way,
but I was having such a fascinating ride that
I couldn't entirely care.

And this full on sensory experience with and without
my senses continued.

I was aware and present in a way I had never known or
had entirely forgotten in this human experience.
I knew and could see ALL.
I was hyper present. I could hear thought and no thought.
I could see all the fractal arrangements.
I could see the beauty in it all.
I could not move fast.
I could not force anything.
I could feel everything.

In that moment I knew everything.
Felt everything.

I was vaguely aware that I didn't care a damn what
anyone might think.
I looked up to the moon and the sky, and the immensity
and intensity of it all, and I felt so.
Fucking. Free.

*All feelings of guilt or anger or responsibility or
obligation were gone.
I didn't feel them toward this person or that person or
even my precious Gaia.
Gone.
I am FREE.*

*Later, I had a similar experience; this time with wholeness.
I noticed that in this state, I no longer wanted for
anything.
I no longer needed anything.
If I had been asked in that moment to part with any of my
material, I would have given it freely.
I had no desire.
I was WHOLE.*

*When I met again with other people, I could feel their
thoughts, their insecurities, their need to prove.
All the stuff I'd spent a lifetime—lifetimes—
attempting to overcome.
Prostrating into frustration.*

*And I knew in that moment that if I stayed in this state of
wholeness and NO THOUGHT and knowing,
I would never be relatable to others again.*

*I had a fleeting bring-back emotion earlier about
this when I realized that it might bring me to
have to part ways with my dear friends.
After all, what could I say when there was
nothing more to say?
What could I possibly "contribute"?
I knew that all I'd ever have to do again would be to just
look within the soul of another to have them "hear" me.
That I would only need a look to know.*

*I could not engage in any level of superficiality.
Idle thoughts were not available to me.
Casual conversation, an impossibility.
So, I went to take a shower.*

*I took the first shower of my life that night.
I knew I didn't need anything called soap.
I didn't need to brush my teeth.
I felt every drop of water caress my body.
When I finally closed the flow of water and took the
Turkish towel in my hands and brought it up to my face,
and felt the warmth generated between my
hands the towel and my face, I sighed out,
"This is why I love to be human."*

*I felt the bed for the first time.
I felt my dressing gowns for the first time.
I was only PRESENCE.
AWARENESS.*

*A fever took over my body that night and
into the entire next day, but no part of me recognized it
as a fever. I could sense a reorganization of my cells.
I could sense groups of them floating upward, like a
flock of birds flying in unison from where they had been
blocked in my body.*

*This continued all day.
I had no desire for food, no desire for company, no
desire.
And again, I knew that if I remained in this state,
I would not be able to return into any kind of "normality",
and I entertained momentarily whether or not
I truly cared about that.*

*In the end, my desire to relate and be relatable
did win, and I slowly started coming "back".
Even if I had been "there" more than ever
before in my life.*

OPEN UP TO FUN, OPEN UP TO YOU

I was very reluctant to share this experience of awakening in this book. I mean, how can I account for it? How can I even begin to describe the ways in which it changed me?

The best I can do is to:

1. Note that relaxing and opening the door to playfulness (or fun) was the only way "in".

    "Unless you become again as a child, you will not enter the kingdom." – Matthew 18:3

2. Say that it's okay to have fun. Your life is meant to be fun. Or in the words of Ram Dass, "It's okay to shovel snow. And it's okay to be happy."

3. Give thanks. I stand on the shoulders of so many giants in my quest for awakening.

    Giants that helped open my eyes: Alan Watts, Oprah, Dr. Joe Dispenza, Ram Dass, Anthony De Mello, Dr. Wayne Dyer, Les Brown, Sarah Blakley, Jim Carrey, and more.

4. Tell you one other secret that allowed me to open up and play with the mysteries of life.

    You can read about it in the next chapter.

For now, take a break, and go have some fun!

CHAPTER 6

Opt Out

"[A] divided mind [is] unstable in all its ways."
– James 1:8

Recently, I saw a post on Instagram with the acronym JOMO (joy of missing out). It's ironic that this "citation" is coming from a place where lots of us go to miss out on our own lives.

Fear of missing out (FOMO) is real. It's primordial. It touches our need to be part of a group—our need for acceptance and approval. When we withdraw from external stimuli, even for just a bit, it can provoke all sorts of uncomfortable chemical responses in the body, just like trying to get off a drug.

Billions are spent annually to capture our attention through screens, billboards, magazines, you name it. The addiction to these stimuli is real. So it takes a lot of willpower (at least initially) to call our attention back to creating inner directed, joyful lives. But it's worth it. Freedom is priceless.

That said, **distraction is a habit best broken slowly.** Incremental withdrawal.

When we intentionally decide to miss out (or opt out of information overload), we can unconsciously wonder, *Will people still like me (if I'm not showing some aspect of my life that validates my worthiness to be liked)? Will I miss out on something great?*

Those questions, or fears, are important, and we'll address them in just a moment. First, let's take a look at the power of a divided mind versus that of a focused, coherent one.

WHAT'S HAPPENING IN YOUR BRAIN?

Most of us are going in and out of four main brainwave frequencies daily, namely: beta, alpha, theta, and delta. Very few of us exercise any conscious direction over these brainwave changes. This chapter is designed to teach you how to be one of the few who does.

Let's look at each one.

BETA: The fragmented, unfocused mind

If you're checking your phone first thing in the morning, I can practically guarantee you that you're in medium to high-range beta most of your day. On a literal note, what that means is that your brainwave frequencies are oscillating between 15 to 30 hertz (Hz), which translates to medium to high levels of anxiety and stress—a kind of cognitive overload that will wear you out quickly. When the brain starts to cool down, you'll move into low beta brainwaves (between 12 to 15 Hz), allowing you to increase focus and feel more relaxed. Generally speaking, however, staying in the "comfort" zone of beta can become very *uncomfortable*.

ALPHA: Chilling out the mind

When we begin to decrease information intake and calm down about missing out, we start to access alpha frequencies. We can easily slip into this type of electrical activity in the brain (8 to 12 Hz) when we listen to certain types of music, when we daydream, or when we do a few minutes of meditation. It's that easy to chill our brains out a bit, and the effect is enormous. On a practical level, this alpha frequency equates to decreased anxiety, increased well-being, and improved cognitive performance. When we're in alpha, it's easier to concentrate and create. We feel happier and more relaxed, which affects how we show up in every area of our life.

THETA: Slowing down to speed up

Theta (frequencies ranging from 4 to 8 Hz) is where things start to get super interesting.

While most people experience theta only as they're coming in and out of dream states, we can trigger this frequency when we are deeply relaxed in playful, creative activity or meditation. This frequency is associated with high levels of intuition and imaginative thought, and is correlated with improved memory consolidation, emotional regulation, and enhanced cognitive performance. Theta is also where we start to get glimpses into our interconnectedness, or what has been called "the unity behind all things." Being in this frequency allows us to directly observe our inherent ability to affect outcomes (more on this below).

DELTA: You're flying (awake in the dream)

As we dive much deeper into relaxed focus—witnessed, for example, when experiencing a kind of single-minded devotion—we begin to access delta frequencies.

These frequencies (0.5 to 4 Hz) are often observed in elite performers or athletes, martial masters, and very experienced meditators. But we all have access to this frequency in states of deep sleep, or REM sleep. This is one of the reasons why it's so important to be mindful of what we expose ourselves to while sleeping or upon waking or falling asleep, because our minds are also easily programmable while in this frequency.

As we increase delta brainwave activity, we enhance immune function, increase tissue repair and regeneration, and improve overall physical and mental health. So avoiding cognitive overload and learning to deeply focus is a kind of fountain of youth.

GO WHERE YOU WANT, FASTER (THE FOUR WAYS OF GETTING ICE CREAM)

Opting out is one of the main secrets to moving into enhanced frequencies—to struggling less and getting where you want to go a lot faster. The most direct way I ever heard this explained was by likening the four frequencies described above to four gears on a race car. Those higher gears—or enhanced frequencies—require less effort from the engine, less fuel, less wear and tear (translation: less stress, less irritability, less frustration and anxiety), the natural result of which is increased mastery and confidence.

The best analogy I've found for understanding these varying states of consciousness was in some amusing banter between Wayne Dyer and Deepak Chopra. They weren't talking about brainwave frequencies, per se, but ever since listening to them, I've found "ways of getting ice cream" to be the best way of understanding and explaining beta, alpha, theta, and delta. What follows is my own interpretation of what they were saying (not the actual discussion).

The first way of getting ice cream: You think* of ice cream, and you decide you're going to go out and get some.

It doesn't matter what time of night it is; you've gotta have that ice cream. So, say it's 3 a.m. and you live in the United States. You drive your car all around until you find a 7-Eleven convenience store. They're selling some freezer burn variety, and you buy it. At this point, you're exhausted and just want to go back to sleep, but you eat the (very unsatisfying) ice cream because you came all that way. Dyer and Chopra didn't take the analogy this far, but bear with me, because this is what medium to high beta can feel like. You're racing all around, trying to *make it happen*. You will eventually get where you're going, but the effort is heavy and unnecessary. It's a kind of searching, restless energy that zaps you of your creativity, flow, and pleasure.

The second way of getting ice cream: You think of ice cream, and you know your roommate Lucy is out in town and wouldn't mind picking up some on her way back.

So you call Lucy, she agrees, and you wait, knowing that the ice cream is on its way. What a marvelous state of relaxed creation: thought → connection → desired outcome. This is like alpha, where you can relax into it, rather than forcing or fretting. It's where you've enlisted someone or something seemingly external to you to help fulfill your desire. It's where you take less action and chill, knowing that the object of your focus is on its way.

The third way of getting ice cream: You think of ice cream, and your boyfriend knocks at your door moments later with flowers and a big tub of the most delicious, gourmet After Eight that you've ever tasted.

You can't believe it when this happens. You tell all your friends about it the next day. It's just like those times that you're merely thinking of someone and they call in that instant. It's such an exciting surprise to know we have this extraordinary capability. This kind of thought-outcome sequence can be likened to the theta state. This is where we begin to access the collective unconscious and the phenomenon known in quantum theory as non-locality, or quantum entanglement—in the simplest terms, our inherent connectedness to all that is.

The fourth way of getting ice cream: You think of ice cream, and the ice cream *just appears*, seemingly out of nowhere.

This can be likened to delta frequencies, in which nothing seems to limit where our consciousness can go or what it can experience. You start to believe that everything is possible for you. Your instinct, or intuition, guides you to one "magical" occurrence after another. You begin to know that you're always exactly where you're meant to be. It can get more practical than that, though. In my own experience, when I've relaxed deeply and set my focus on something that I've misplaced, for example, it appears exactly where I was looking before and not finding it (when my focus was less relaxed and more fragmented).

I'm using the term "think" very loosely. We do not know the origin of thought and very few of us are consciously directing it. So, unless we're in those more expansive frequencies, it is more accurate to say that the thought impulse emerges in our conscious, i.e., we become aware of the electrical impulse we identify in this example as ice cream.

HOW CAN THE ICE CREAM JUST APPEAR? (GIVE ME MORE OF THAT, PLEASE)

Let's look at how we can enjoy more of that yummy gelato without having to drive all night for it.

We'll start by briefly examining the nature of attention itself. Your attention is like the paparazzi. It instinctively wants to go where the action is the hottest.

If you get slapped across the face, for example, where do you think your attention—*all of your attention*—is going to go? Straight to that slap. It's the "loudest" contender in that moment. It's hot. All your blood is rushing there. It focuses your attention in an instant.

You could just experience the physical sensations of that slap and stop there. But most of us don't. After your physical attention has become so absorbed, what comes next? That's right, your mental attention. *Where the hell did that come from? It's on like Donkey Kong!* Next thing you know, you're straight up brawling and don't know whose hands are whose.

Now, since most of us aren't dealing with literal slaps, let's imagine it's a figurative slap. Someone calls you stupid or lazy. You could just notice the comment and drop it there, as most great masters admonish us to, but yikes if that doesn't feel just like a real slap. Your energy and attention rush to the event, as if you'd been struck. And another kind of brawl begins. This is the worst kind of brawl because it takes over your mind and can go on for hours or days or even years, if unchecked. The more attention you give it, the more difficult to extricate yourself from it.

So, if focused attention is such a powerful force, why are so few of us able to consciously direct it? The simplest answer is that we have not been trained to do so. Indeed, the onslaught of information coming at us at all times, being filtered through our senses and interpreted by our nerves, is so overwhelming that it's a wonder our brains can keep up at all. Let's look at how we can give our brains a break.

The first key to training the mind (Opt Out suggestion #1): Limit information intake.

The clearest takeaway from this understanding of how our attention works is to *limit the noise*. There's this Zen saying I love: *It's the space between the bars that holds the tiger, and the silence between the notes that makes the music.* We've got to give ourselves that silence, that space, if we want to be able to hear our own music—the formless that wants to be expressed through the form.

Here are some of the ways to limit cognitive overload so you can hear and focus on your own dreams and creative impulses:

1. **Turn off data on your phone** (settings → mobile data → slide to "off" mode). This is what I do when I'm in hyper-focus mode. Regular calls can still come in (hardly anyone ever calls anymore, unless it's really important), but you will not receive any other annoying notifications for the time you've set aside for what we covered in Chapters 3 through 5.

2. **Turn off app notifications**. If you really want to get down to business, you can go into each app

you're using and deactivate all notifications. This means you will no longer receive any pings, badges, sounds, and whatever other ways the app keeps you hooked. Turning off notifications is not for the faint of heart. But even if it's hard at first (maybe only try this with the most distracting app to start), the rewards in terms of recuperating your focus, time, and peace of mind are exponential.

3. **Safeguard early morning and late evening blocks of time**. Use this time to daydream, meditate, and take concrete actions that reinforce the in-love-with-life person you're becoming. As we saw above, when you're coming in and out of sleep is when your mind is most programmable, so these times are prime real estate for your dreams.

I know that this kind of radical reclaiming of your freedom isn't easy, but it is *simple*.

Dog → Bell → Salivation. No thank you. You're stronger than that.

The examples above are just to get you started. You'll find your own. That's the fun part. You're playing David vs. Goliath with the forces that are currently vying for your attention—your most precious resource—and we all know David ultimately wins. Reclaim your attention. Use it for *your* dreams, not someone else's.

**The second key to training the mind
(Opt Out suggestion #2): Drop the hot potato.**

Yesterday, I was out walking in the woods. Ahead of me, I saw a young, mustached man with a dog arguing with an older, olive toned woman. They were really going at it. As I got closer, the arguing stopped and both huffed off in opposite directions. I continued my walk until I came upon the young man again; he had stopped to meet a woman who seemed to be his girlfriend. By now he was super heated and telling the tale in vivid detail: "That woman" (*quella signora*) had told him to put a leash on his dog and even came toward the dog with a stick. His energy was furious. His friend joined the spin and also began raging against the older woman…*who was no longer there.*

See how easy it can be? Something shocking strikes. And instead of simply observing and freeing ourselves in that moment, we keep slapping ourselves.

What if instead of engaging with the woman with the stick, the young man had simply pulled his dog close and made some gesture of noting her point, releasing and letting the moment of tension and frustration fade, before heading back off on his own way to meet and have fun with his friend? I wonder…

I also recognize this isn't all that easy, especially because our attention loves to get fixated on the steamiest events. This young guy, for example, probably told that story to many other people that day (and *re-lived* it every time). But is focusing our attention in this sort of way worth our freedom and peace of mind? I don't think so.

Imagine you grab a steaming hot potato out of the oven with your bare hands. What would you do with it? Hold it there until you get a second-degree burn? I certainly hope not. You'd drop that thing without even thinking twice. I know it seems really hard since most of us have been trained to do the opposite with hot "mind" potatoes. But, again, it's your freedom and your dreams. You get to decide.

I say, drop it.

OTHER WAYS WE GET IN OUR WAY (AND CAN STOP)

Now that we've covered a couple of mind training practices, let's briefly look at some other reasons we often find it difficult to opt out of what everyone else is doing and get on with building our own dreams: 1) FOMO and 2) stressing out about things we have absolutely no control over.

What happens when we're always looking for the "next best thing" (translation: FOMO)

Recently at Mindvalley University, where I was a speaker, I met a woman who introduced herself in the food truck line. It was super refreshing how open and curious she was, and we grabbed lunch and spent the next thirty minutes eating and swapping stories. Occasionally throughout our conversation, I noticed she would be looking around and not actively listening or engaging. Then, when we'd finished eating our lunch, I could sense her anxiety to move on to the next thing.

She abruptly switched topic without seeming to notice. Her eyes darted all around, she looked at her phone, and then said she had to run off to get a front row seat at the next talk. She said she would like to save one for me too, but she had already put her stuff on a front row chair and was sure the others were already taken. I smiled and wished her a fun session. Meanwhile, I continued to enjoy the sun on my face and the chatterings all around me, eventually making my way to the empty back row of that same talk.

Later, this woman discovered I was a speaker at the event. She apologized for rushing off before and cutting us off and asked if she could "pick my brain" about, well, everything. She had also done some Instagram "research" and saw that I'd met and spent time with

Richard Branson on his private island, Necker, where I was giving a talk at a global leadership event. She wanted to know all about that too and how she might be able to create a similar opportunity in her life.

You can guess how long that conversation lasted. Not because I didn't want to help—I'm always eager to share where I feel I can add value. The reason we didn't go much further was because this woman's attention was too scattered to receive the insights she was seeking.

Now, just to be clear, I'm not knocking her at all. I get what it's like to fear missing out on something or to go through phases in life when we're more opportunistic. The point is that when we do this, we miss out on what's right in front of us: Life, offering us beautiful opportunity after beautiful opportunity to learn and grow.

What happens when we start trusting life (translation: when we stop stressing out about things we have absolutely no control over)

The actor-artist-author Jim Carrey once said, "When I say life is working for me, I don't really know if that's true. I'm just choosing to believe it's true so that I can deal with things in the best way possible." Such simple advice. It reminds me of Einstein's friendly warning that the most important decision we make in life is whether to believe that we live in a friendly or hostile universe.

What if, for the sake of personal sanity, we just decide that the universe is friendly? What if we open the compartments in our mind that hold the ideas around how everything *should* be (for us to feel comfortable) and just let all those constructs fly away? I know this is scary. I mean, all those neatly arranged ideas are what we created in the first place to give us a sense of security and stability.

But what if they just get us into trouble? What if, as we saw in Chapter 1, what we're trying to control ends up controlling us? When we're stressing about every little thing, we inevitably miss out on the magic. When we choose to believe instead that life is working out for us, that everything is rigged in our favor, as Oprah puts it, we begin to signal our environment accordingly.

The truth is, we have absolutely *zero* control over Life. It does what it wants. All we get to decide is if we're going to let it do its thing, while we stay open and willing to enjoy whatever that is.

When we release control and open like this, we can simply marvel at the epic production as it unfolds. This is freedom. Ironically, it's also the point at which life truly *does* seem to be working for us, as if the waves that once crushed us now lift us up higher and higher.

The only way I've found to consistently step into this magnificence is to get quiet and learn to be fully present with yourself and others, which means opting out so you can *opt in* to your own life. This is where we start to discover JOMO and what it means to live by design, rather than default. Let's talk about that design now.

CHAPTER 7

Live by Design

As you start to win your attention back, your relationship with time will also change. You'll seem to have more of it, and you'll become increasingly aware of the things only you can do to embody the vision you have for yourself and for your life.

Each step in the direction of who you've *decided* to be will help clarify what priorities support it. These are actions, activities, and perception shifts that you cannot delegate to anyone else. If you decide to be physically fit, for example, you cannot outsource exercising your body. You might be able to have someone prepare healthy meals, but that person will not be able to eat them for you. You get the point.

So, who do you want to be? And what actions, activities, and perception shifts belong to that kind of person?

In the previous chapter, we looked at how to free up energy and space for you to begin to consider a higher vision for yourself. When there's less noise blocking your inner guidance, what do you hear? What do you see for yourself? What potentials excite you? What facets of your being have you ignored or overridden in the name of expediency or distraction? What have you been doing that you don't need to be doing?

Once you get quiet enough, the answers will come. Then comes the fun part: acting on them.

HOW TO RECLAIM YOUR TIME

Often what keeps us from taking action is the belief that we have to have a super clear vision for our life in order to move forward. This is simply untrue. Just notice what's calling most to you right now. And then act on it. Even the tiniest action will stoke the flame.

But wait—what if you don't even know what's calling most? What if everything around you seems to be vying equally for your time and attention? Take the dog for a walk, see if someone commented on your post from yesterday, go to the gym, call your mom… How do you figure out what to focus on first?

If your vision for yourself isn't all that clear yet (and even if it is), the following time training will help lessen the noise and clear your mind long enough to discern what *really* needs your attention now.

The four dimensions we'll cover below are a mashup of models I studied in leadership training at Vanity Fair Corporation and time lessons I learned from Steven Covey and Tony Robbins. It's the best way I've found so far to explain how some people seem to have lots more time than others. It also overlaps somewhat with the ice cream analogy we covered in the last chapter.

Before reading any further, grab a sheet of paper and draw four concentric circles that fill up the whole page. Trust me. What we're about to cover will completely flip your relationship with time and free up gobs of it. But you kinda have to see what I'm talking about to get the full picture.

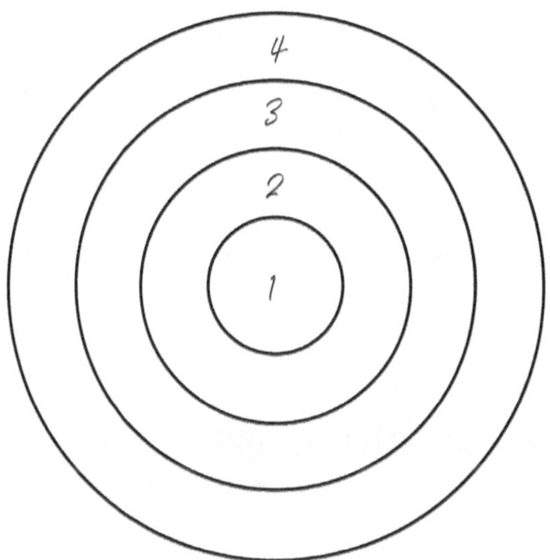

The Dimension of Distraction: Where did all the time go?

Okay, now that you've drawn your circles, label the outermost one the "Dimension of Distraction". Below or next to that, you can write: *not important, not urgent stuff*. When your time is being consumed by this dimension, you're spinning your wheels, going nowhere fast (like high beta).

For most of us, a great example of the Dimension of Distraction is social media. You're scrolling, scrolling… Yikes! Half an hour or an hour later, you don't feel that great, and you wonder how the heck you (or, rather your attention) stayed put there for that long. It's the same sort of yucky feeling we get after eating that 7-Eleven ice cream at three in the morning.

A little note before we move on to the next circle: None of these dimensions is bad *per se*. What's important is to clearly see the time we're dedicating to each one and how we can reproportion things to master our attention and, hence, our fate.

The Dimension of Delusion: Who's running the show?

Label the next circle inward on your drawing the "Dimension of Delusion", and under or next to that label, add the note: *seemingly urgent, but not important* (at least not to you). This time dimension is where you're being sucked into other people's priorities. It's the email you get from Pete right after your morning coffee that says he needs a document *pronto*.

This dimension typically feels slightly better than "distraction" because your focus levels are increased (low beta frequency), and you'll also experience a little hit of dopamine (spiked momentarily by feeling needed), but ultimately, it will drain your energy and possibly create a bit of resentment, if allowed to run the show. It's where you prioritize what's important to others, rather than what's important to you.

Again, sometimes we need to be in this dimension. The question is when and how much?

The Dimension of Demand: Recipe for burnout.

The next circle in your diagram is the "Dimension of Demand"—this stuff is *important and urgent*. If you get a call right now telling you someone you love is in the hospital, you're going to drop this book and run for the door. This is demand. It's unignorable.

The problem is that many of us—especially high performers—have lumped way too many things in this dimension. When we live primarily in this dimension and convince ourselves that most of our actions are urgent and important, we activate the hormones of stress. If we make this our default state, we're looking at premature aging, metabolic dysfunction, and persistent anxiety, to name a few of its rough side effects.

Sometimes life will land us in this dimension, and we don't get to decide. Other times, we can decide that we're not going to make everything such a big deal. We can ditch the "urgent" part and get much more creative with it all.

The Dimension of Design: Consciously creating a meaningful life.

What if we could harness the kind of focus that "demand" gives us without getting stressed by it? What if we could fully place our attention on our creative intentions and watch them come to life as a result? We can. This is where the ice cream just shows up.

It's the central circle in your diagram—what Tony Robbins calls the "bullseye"—and what I call the "Dimension of Design"—where we're focused on the *important, not urgent stuff*. The actions that live here are the ones that will provide the most leverage for your vision because they are the ones only you can take.

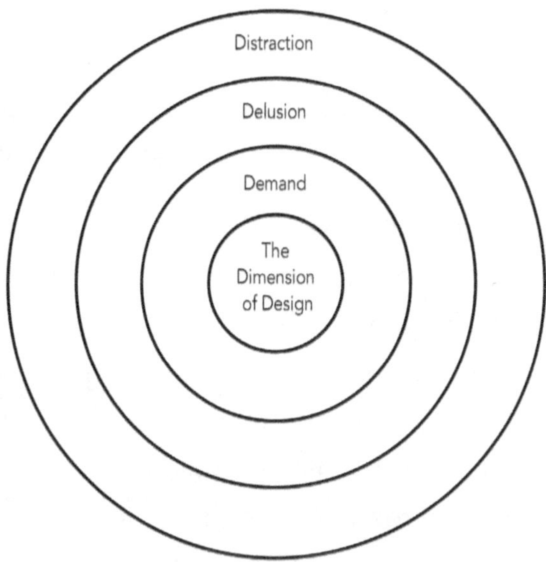

As we train our awareness to keep returning to this dimension, we free up untold amounts of time. We seem to accomplish the impossible. Other people marvel at how we've changed physically or professionally. And it was all the very simple result of placing our primary attention on what we were previously putting off, but what we've always known was vitally important.

When we're in this dimension we're playing, and life loves play. Life is play.

RELAX AND MAKE UP A FUN LIFE FOR YOURSELF

Back when I was working as a corporate executive, I used to hastily eat my lunch in front of my computer, while clicking through dozens of emails. My mornings and afternoons would be filled rushing from meeting to meeting, reviewing reports, taking calls, and putting out random fires all over the place. I believed all that meant I was an Important Person.

Because that's what Important People do, right? They keep "busy". They're simultaneously talking to a client, writing an email to their assistant, clicking between the multiple tabs open on their computer, and nodding to a colleague who pops into the office, flashing a report that they need to read. And in the evenings, they're so depleted that they crave a dose of "distraction" (alcohol, TV, an excess of food) as a break from all the stress.

Playing this Busy Important Person role can be interesting for a bit. The adrenaline rush we get from the perceived demand and the endorphin hits that come from feeling needed by others can give us a momentary sense of satisfaction. But, while it's tempting to glorify "busy" and become dependent on Pavlovian prompts (e.g., app/text notifications on our phones, email boxes full of other people's priorities, etc.), it's also a recipe for feeling frustrated and far away from the life we envision for ourselves. Being stuck in "demand" or "delusion" (and then self-medicating with "distraction") isn't nearly as compelling as the prolonged satisfaction that comes from dropping out of that race and into a life of design.

The first time I glimpsed the power of the Dimension of Design was back at my corporate job, eating that sandwich in front of my computer. Maybe it was the stomach acid or something deeper inside me, but I decided to get up from my desk, exit the building, and take a walk around the block. When I came back, I was feeling so refreshed that I decided to close my door, pull down the blinds on my windows, and do what I'd been putting off forever: I meditated. It was only for a few minutes, but after that I felt so great that I decided to avoid the trappings of my inbox and pull out some project work I'd also been putting off for way too long.

My mind was so relaxed, focused, and creative in that moment that I easily and joyfully discovered solutions and ideas that ended up adding a lot to my company's bottom line. This was the perfect example of opting out so I could come back stronger, more creative, and more impactful—*design over default*.

Now I use the Dimension of Design for my own business—to write this book you're holding, for example, or to help my clients generate millions doing what they love.

How do you want to use it?

WHAT'S *YOUR* DEFAULT DIMENSION?

Now that you're familiar with the different time dimensions available to you, consider this question: How much time are you currently spending in each one? The point behind answering this question is not to feel bad about where you might be placing (or misplacing) your attention; the point is to become aware of how you're currently directing this precious resource and to reallocate it to a life by design.

For most of us, the day passes by in a kind of blur. **We aren't paying attention to our attention.** But if our attention is what brings the specific potentials or probability outcomes to life, then there's no way around noticing where it's going, and redirecting it where needed, if we want to live better.

Awareness is the first step. What's your default at the moment? Are you living in distraction, delusion, demand? Or are you already in design a lot of the time and just want to amp it up?

You'll likely notice some resistance as you move your attention to the Dimension of Design stuff. That's because until we master this, our attention wants to go where the noise is the loudest. That's okay. Just gently guide it back. Setting up little reminders throughout your day can help you notice and pivot.

The idea is to make it as easy as possible to act on what's important to you *before* getting to all the rest, which will paradoxically make "all the rest" a lot easier to manage and digest.

SETTING A NEW DEFAULT

Imagine that when you wake up every morning, you're given a full tank of energy to use for that day. Every experience you have—anything you think, do, say, feel—requires some of that energy. You can replenish your tank throughout your day with naps or meditation or a relaxed walk in the park, but your reserves will still be highest when your tank is full.

What this means is that the best time of day to focus on the Dimension of Design—important-not-urgent stuff— is right at the start of your day.

This is where most of us miss the boat. We promise ourselves that we'll get to the exercise or the writing or the meditation or the [*insert the thing you know you should prioritize but don't]* later. We'll make time for it *after* we check our email or watch the news or just take a quick peek at our Instagram feed. Boom. Right there we lost the little window into momentum.

It's not worth it. And the funny thing is we only have to delay those little dopamine hits for a few minutes each day to start gaining ground on the life we want. It's a practice. The trick is to go about it slowly. Right at the start of your day, devote ten minutes (or even five) to focus on your top priority. Do this for a month and you'll start craving more. Because you'll see the results.

Test it out for yourself: Take meditation, for example, a practice that will supercharge everything else in your life. Give it five minutes first thing in the morning for one month and watch as this new frequency frees up pockets of time you never thought you had and enhances your creativity in ways that will astonish you.

PARETO AND PARKINSON: TWO PRINCIPLES THAT CAN HELP

There are a couple other time-action principles you'll need to know to accelerate your life by design: The Pareto Principle and Parkinson's Law.

You're likely already familiar with the Pareto Principle, or the 80/20 rule, as it's more commonly called. Simply put, it's the idea that 80 percent of your results come from 20 percent of your actions. In my experience working with the highest performers in the world, the more you cultivate clarity around who you want to be and the life you're committed to consciously designing, that rule is more like 90/10, or even 95/5. That is, you can put in 5 percent effort for 95 percent of your gain, if you focus on that last dimension!

This principle reminds me of the brilliant sentiment attributed to Archimedes: "Give me a lever long enough and a fulcrum on which to place it, and I shall move the world." Translated: What can you leverage? What skills and talents can *only you* express? What is better left to others (or at least left off your daily schedule)?

Certain actions, activities, or practices will provide enormous leverage for you. Your job is to figure out what those are. Does spending time on TikTok move your needle? Maybe it does, if that's where you're inspiring millions of people. If not, take that same daily time and pour it into writing that book you know is in you, or learning a new language so you can reach millions more people with your gifts.

Start today (there's no better time): What are the one to three actions you know will propel you into a life by design? Ease in slowly, consistently prioritizing these actions early in the day for the next month. As you get better and better at this linear movement in the direction of your dreams, a non-linear force will show up to aid you in your endeavors. Your efforts will be compounding and miracles will begin to materialize. You've got the lever, and you're moving the world.

While you're applying pressure to the lever of your dreams, there's one other time-action principle to keep in mind, and that is Parkinson's Law, or the idea that work expands to fill the time allotted for its completion. When we determine ahead of time how long something will take to complete or how much time we will give it, the mind helps keep us on that track. The more we practice this, the easier it becomes to focus in bursts, and the more prolific we become.

This book you're holding (or listening to) is also thanks to Pareto and Parkinson. Writing is a major lever for my life's vision. It's an action I take (almost) daily, since I dream it will result in inspiring you to live the life you want. And instead of opening a potentially endless void for this book's completion, I use Parkinson's insight to focus on completing one chapter every week. That time allocation is ambitious for me, but it's keeping me mostly on point.

Give it a shot yourself: Can you commit to twenty-minute bursts of concentration every weekday to begin bringing your dreams to life? As you do, you'll discover a great paradox: Time discipline leads to time freedom. Enjoy!

WHEN ALL ELSE FAILS

Right about now, you might be telling me off in your head: *Okay, Cort, I get all this you're saying about time and prioritizing what's important to me...but I still can't seem to get my butt in motion around what I know I need to be doing.*

If that's the case, the only solution is to literally move your butt. Stop reading this book. Get your gorgeous derriere up and dance, roll around, go for a walk in the woods. Just move! Trust me on this one. Most of the time what we refer to as a "creative block" is simply stuck, stagnant energy in our physical body.

The fastest way to free up the energy required for new actions is to release that stuckness through movement.

Have you ever noticed those times when you've been sitting at your computer for a while, struggling to figure something out, and then you get up for a few minutes and the answer comes? This is because even the smallest physical reset will help you refocus your attention and energy. Paradoxically, the more movement you allow, the more focused stillness will arise.

At first, breaking up concentration with movement *so you can get back to concentration* might feel unnatural. This is because our very natural tendency to move our bodies has been stifled. Growing up, most of us are admonished *thousands of times* to "sit still!" In the classroom, the living room, at the kitchen table, in the car, we're told over and over to stop moving so much. Stop rolling around and curling up and splaying out. Just STOP.

Well, this is an invitation to START again.

Just because we didn't have permission while we were growing up, doesn't mean that those (mostly well-meaning) adults knew what they were doing when they tried to "calm us down".

Calm down. Dim your light. Stop being soooo much.

Limit your fluidity. Block your truth.

Not anymore. No thank you.

Sitting here writing to you, I'm "chair dancing" to John Mayer's song "New Light". My feet are bouncing on the ground, and I'm rotating my thighs and hips on one of those disc cushions. It feels so good to let my hips and shoulders and my belly move in waves. Even if I'm still in a somewhat constricted typing position, I feel freer than those times when I used to sit stock-still.

I've even started moving like this in my meditations. Tuning into my body and the way the breath moves through it, pockets where it feels like energy is trapped—allowing all that has been blocking the flow of energy to be released, so that I can get back to the formless and how it wants to express itself through this form.

This is an invitation for you to do the same. The more you move, the more you will be able to choose a life by design. When you step into this fluid dance with life, you begin to free the light within—the light that is waiting to spread out on the scene like a giant star.

That light will lead you straight to an unshakeable confidence. Which is what we're covering in the next chapter.

CHAPTER 8

Be Confident

Once you commit to living by design—prioritizing what's important to *you*—another phenomenon emerges: You start to trust more in where life is taking you. It begins to feel as if life is *living you*. You release even more control (or the illusion of control) and relax into the belief that everything is rigged in your favor.

This is what it means to be confident.

Confidence is not about being the most outspoken or flamboyant person in the room. You don't have to be the strongest, the fastest, the loudest, the most persuasive, or any of the other traits we are normally told a confident person possesses. Confidence isn't boastful or arrogant. It has nothing to do with titles or positions. Confidence (from the Latin *confidere*) means trust or full reliance. It's what happens when we decide to trust in life's unfolding, and to lend our skills and talents to that unfolding in the best way we can. Once we make this agreement with life, a deep-seated peace begins to emerge within us, and we embody a kind of ecstasy or inner bliss that is available to all of us.

There's a parable I love to tell to illustrate what is meant by this kind of confidence. I've tweaked it here to also share the secret to prosperity of every kind.

GOOD? BAD? WHO KNOWS?

One day, a farmer who lived near a small village lost his horse. It escaped into the surrounding woods, where it was unlikely to be found.

When the villagers heard of this misfortune they came to sympathize with the farmer. *Poor guy...lost his only horse. What will he and his son do now?* This was a *bad* thing.

Instead of commiserating with the villagers, the farmer simply remarked: "I give thanks to Life."

Whaaat? This confused the villagers terribly. But maybe he was just in shock. They accepted the farmer's momentary madness and went on their way.

The next day, the farmer's son went looking for the lost horse in the woods and found not only that horse, but another one in its company. The son was able to steer both of the animals safely back to the farm.

When the villagers got wind of this turn of events, they were instantly back at the farmer's door, where they heartily congratulated him on his gain. *What a lucky guy. What* good *fortune.* The farmer's simple response was, once again, "I give thanks to Life." *Of course he's giving thanks,* the villagers thought, *he's a rich man now. No one has two horses…*

A few days later, while training the new horse, the farmer's son fell off its back and broke his leg. When this news spread, the villagers came knocking once again. *You poor, poor man. First you lose your horse, and now this. What are you going to do now that your son is unable to work and tend the fields? You are too old to manage this farm.* The farmer gently smiled and responded, "I give thanks to Life," and said no more.

It was clear now to the villagers that the old man had completely lost his senses. What in the world did he have to give thanks for? He clearly didn't understand the magnitude of his son's injury. But they couldn't convince the farmer that this was bad, so they went on their way.

A week later all the villagers were in a frenzy. A consignment officer had come to the village and was drafting all the young men into war. The officer couldn't take the farmer's son due to the broken leg. And, well, you know how the rest of the story goes…

In the original parable, it is said that the farmer responded with something along the lines of, "Good? Bad? Who knows?" This is also a very powerful stance. Because the truth is, *we don't know.* And when we relax into the not-knowing with a kind of open curiosity, we free ourselves from the toxicity of labeling and judging life's unfolding. The events are just that. Events. Or as Shakespeare put it in *Hamlet*, "nothing neither good nor bad, but thinking makes it so."

Okay, so you might be wondering how we apply this confidence, or trust, when the spiral of "this is bad" thoughts start to take over. How can we choose gratitude instead? How does choosing gratitude make us more confident? And, in general, what makes gratitude so powerful?

Let's start with the spinning, spiraling thoughts and what we can do about them.

LEARN TO THINK AND GROW RICH

Did you know that with all the advances in neuroscience, we still do not know where thoughts come from? There isn't a part of the brain we can point to—say, for example, the prefrontal cortex—to indicate where thought originates. What we do know is that thoughts are electrical impulses that sort of "flash" into our consciousness, and that most of us are having about 50,000 to 70,000 of these thought impulses a day.

We also know that the average human is cycling the same or similar 50,000 to 70,000 thoughts through his or her consciousness *every day*. Those thought formations are informing matter. And, again, they're mostly automatic…a kind of unconscious brainwashing or molding of information to create your environment, both internal and external.

For example, the thought impulse "I am sick", when accompanied by a steady emotional charge, affects the chemical responses and biological processes in your body. In brain-body scans, we can witness how the repetition (or attachment) to this kind of thought impulse releases neuropeptides (or chemical messengers from the brain's neurons) that can wreak havoc around the tissues of our body's organs.

I'm not a neuroscientist or an expert on any of this, but I've seen some of those scans and they've reinforced my dedication to being a human who knows *how to think*. Because the truth is, you and everything you perceive around you is merely an arrangement of information, i.e., thought patterns. Therefore, a different arrangement of information results in a different reality.

One of the all-time most sold books on this topic is Napoleon Hill's *Think and Grow Rich*. I used to wonder,

If millions of people around the world are reading this and not getting rich, what are they missing? And then it struck me: There are two words implicit in that title that will change everything for you once you get them, and those are "learn to" think.

Which of those floating electrical impulses are you holding onto? Which ones have you decided will not make it through the net? The ones you're using to define you? What if you could let them go? What if you could begin to train your mind to consciously manufacture a thought of your choosing and then hold that thought until the energy momentum behind it is such that your physical body and environment begin to take on the quality of that thought?

This kind of mastery is no joke. It's the hardest work in the world. That's why so few people ever bother with it. But if you do decide to master this "game" of learning how to think—consciously directing thought toward a specific probability outcome until it takes shape—you and your life can take on any form you wish. I mean, after all, if you're just an arrangement of information, why not arrange things in a way that is appealing to you?

Once you enjoy the fruits of that for a while, an even greater potential opens up to you.

You begin to wonder what would happen if you let *all* thoughts through… If you stop identifying with the ones you've chosen to *inform the form* and instead you just observe the thought/information-formations all around you, without labels or judgment.

This is very difficult (and scary) at first. Because you've expended so much effort up to this point—first *unconsciously* directing the nature of reality (or form), and then *consciously* directing it—that giving up the game all together will feel radically unfamiliar and destabilizing. The idea alone can provoke an almost paralyzing fear.

What are you without the thought?

Let's wait to jump down that rabbit hole. First, let's understand more about how to train our minds to direct thought.

BEGIN TO TRAIN THE MIND

Let's look a little closer at what the parable of the farmer teaches us about the nature of thought and how to start consciously observing and directing it.

Let's say the villagers represent the mind itself, with its tendency to judge and spin narrative around life's events. When the farmer encounters these "villagers" (or thought spins), how does he react, or rather *respond* to them?

Does the farmer engage in the narrative, or thought spin? No.
Does the farmer stop working? No.
Does the farmer change his tactics to attempt to affect a different outcome? No.
Does the farmer even consider wanting something else? Who knows?

Maybe on some level the farmer doesn't like what's happening, but he *chooses* to avoid labeling any of it. He simply allows the experience to be the experience. Nothing more. He's aware of the event and the resultant perception, but he doesn't cling to either. *Good? Bad? Who knows?*

In this way, Life can flow freely through him because he is not denying or grasping at any of it. This is what it means to be free.

In my alternative version, I like to believe that the farmer chooses freedom *and* joy. By giving thanks for every-thing, he can bliss out on all of it. He knows (or decides) that it's all perfect.

Okay, so how does this parable translate to everyday life and what can we do or practice once those "villagers" (thought concepts within and around us) seem to be taking over and threatening our peace of mind? What steps can we take to start changing our relationship with the nature of thought?

First: Whatever you do, don't blame yourself for the thought. As we saw above, we don't even know where thought impulses come from. It's not your fault the villagers showed up on your doorstep. They simply showed up, and it doesn't have to be a huge deal.

Second: Now that you're more relaxed about the presence of these thoughts (they're just villagers passing by for a chat before going on their way) notice if you can relax even deeper, breathing right into your heart as you simply notice or watch the thoughts.

Third: Once you leave aside blame or shame (they're just thoughts), and you relax your heart around these temporary visitors, you get to decide how long the villagers will linger—whether or not to accept or propagate any given idea. You can invite them to stay and party, noticing how entertaining they are, or you can watch them leave your porch in search of more willing conspirators.

It becomes fun. It becomes a game. At this point you are changing your relationship with the very nature of thought itself. If you want to let go of the thought, to let it move through your awareness without any snags, simply continue to breathe into your heart. Relax your shoulders as you do this and just repeat, "Thank You." Or at least that's how I like to do it. You'll find your own way of softening around the thought so that it can change form or disappear.

When you start to master thought in these ways, you inherit the kingdom; you open to the riches that were always available to you. You discover that your peace of mind, your happiness, your sense of abundance were never dependent on situations, events, people, or things. You are no longer as A.E. Housman put it, "a stranger and afraid in a world I never made." You can watch life's unfolding with total trust—true confidence.

WHAT? MY PASSPORT IS EXPIRED??

As soon as travel restrictions were lifted post-pandemic, I was booked on the first flight I could get to the States. I was aching to see my friends and family and also really excited about working face-to-face with people again. A few days after my scheduled arrival, I was set to give a talk in Miami to fifty-plus Chambers of Commerce, and then travel on to a number of smaller workshops and conferences that were spread out coast to coast for my time there.

Only problem was, my U.S. passport had expired during the pandemic, and I didn't notice until two days before my departure. Eek. My mind raced to any possible way to remedy the situation. Every idea that emerged was a no-go. It would have been physically impossible to travel to and from Milan before leaving, even if I was somehow miraculously able to procure an appointment with the Embassy, and there wouldn't be enough time to process the document, even if I did have an extra day and could get the appointment. It also wasn't possible to travel on my Italian passport, which was still valid, because U.S. citizens have to enter the country with a U.S. passport.

I knew all that. There wasn't anything I could *do*, so I decided to relax. Instead of letting the spiral of thoughts (*I could have/should have* etc.) completely overtake me, I just let it be what it was. I rested in the peace of not having to figure it out and the knowing that it was all okay—even if I wasn't permitted to go. When I was in that relaxed state, a nudge kept coming to me: "Go to the airport anyway. Just go and see."

So on the appointed travel day, I took the hour and a half trek to the airport to see what would happen. When I arrived at the check-in counter, I explained that my passport had expired during the pandemic and that I only realized a couple of days ago. I still had a valid Italian passport, so maybe I could travel with that? The answer was a decisive NO. I needed a valid U.S. passport to enter my country.

As I looked into the eyes of the airline attendant, I felt a deep peace enter my body, and for whatever reason, I asked one more time: "Are you sure it's not possible for me to take this trip?" She took a breath and seemed to visibly relax. She said she would go and ask her supervisor, but quickly added that she didn't think it would be possible.

As she went to speak with her supervisor, I found myself praying. I wasn't praying for things to go "my way"—as I would have a few years before. Instead, I was asking for peace and joy at any outcome. I wanted to feel totally serene no matter where life was taking me—back to my home in Italy or onward to my home in the U.S.

When the flight attendant came back, I was in such a state of peace that I was almost ecstatic. She could have told me I was going to Timbuktu and I would have been equally excited and open to it. My mind and heart were filled with an overwhelming sense of gratitude for exactly where I was, physically and in my own psyche.

I often wonder if embodying that state is what led to what happened next. I'll never know. But when she returned, she asked me if I had any other document that proved that I was a current U.S. citizen. I had my driver's license, which was also expired (lol) and I also happened to have a very worn piece of paper from the U.S. Transportation Security Administration with my Known Traveler Number, which was valid for the next couple of years. "Could these work?" I asked. She took them off with her again, saying, "Let me see."

She returned with photocopies of the documents for me to sign and a smile that said, "You're going to America." She printed out the ticket and wished me a fantastic trip. Her countenance had changed so much from when I first approached her at check-in that I imagined that the peace I felt made its way directly into her heart too. I thanked her with a conspiratorial smile and was on my way.

Two more times on the trip—once in France and again at customs in the U.S.—I was stopped and thought I might not make it after all. Both times, I relaxed into my heart, breathing straight into the peace of accepting events and people and thoughts as they are. Not wanting to change any of it. And, again, such gratefulness took over my being that, no matter what the final outcome, I was happy and trusting.

If I told you what happened with the U.S. customs officer and how I made it through that final checkpoint, you probably wouldn't believe me. I'll save that story for when we meet, dear reader.

For now, all I can add to this is: If *I*, someone who was riddled for so long with anxiety and overthinking and a tendency to try to control everything, was able to arrive at these states of inner peace and bliss, then you most definitely can too.

FINDING CONFIDENCE AND
LEAVING THE CAGE

If you're open, you trust. If you trust, you're confident.

So how can we open? And how can we stay open? The fastest way I've found is through the breath. Bring the breath into those constricted, tight places. Use it to open. You are meant to stay open. You are meant to trust. It *is* all happening for you. I know it's hard to believe that. I know that when something sparks pain, you want to close. I know that you want to draw back. I know that you want the bars around you so you can feel a little safe. But would you rather be facing that perceived danger from inside a cage or out in the open, where at least you have a chance to fly away or face it and let your courage define a new you?

How does one get out of the cage?

You built it. You know its structure. You can go back in whenever you want. It's not a physical place. It's all your fears. Those are the bars. The cage itself is a concept, an intricate concept of the mind. When you sense the tightness, the constriction of that mental cage, look up. Breathe. Direct your attention away from or just beyond your fears. There's so much light and love out there, just right past the edges of your terror of opening up and letting go.

This kind of trust and openness to all of life leads to a joyful serenity. It's a *happiness* that passes all understanding. And this is precisely where we're going next—the seemingly elusive, yet ever present truth of happiness.

Be Happy

Just as confidence flows from trust—trust in yourself, trust in others, and trust in life—happiness also arises from this kind of openness and faith. It might not always "look" like happiness, though. Some of our darkest moments hold a beauty that would fill us with tears of appreciation if we would only have the courage to be fully present with them.

One morning at a local café, a woman spontaneously began speaking with me. She described herself as an empath and said, "You give me a good feeling. I can tell I can talk to you." In the next few minutes, she shared so much about her life, including how the death of her mom five years prior had changed everything for her. She explained that she used to be so happy, but now she couldn't be happy anymore. It was too devastating for her.

Listening to her made me want to cry—less for the pain that she was certainly still feeling than for the beauty that inspired all that pain. Here she was, sitting on a gold mine of love. The love that binds a mother to her child and a child to her mother. A love that is the source of so much joy, if we will only allow ourselves to connect to it, in whatever form it takes.

This is scary—to see and connect with the beauty that can only be known in suffering. But when we have the courage to dive into the pain, rather than resisting or negating it, we find a kind of pure truth, an innocence and a clarity that lives behind every rusty hinge of our existence up to that point.

And when we shine the light of our open awareness there, we can heal and grow.

YOU DON'T HAVE TO SMILE TO BE HAPPY

Sadness, tears, anger, and all the other emotions we label as "unhappy" can be so uncomfortable for ourselves and especially for others. That discomfort most often leads to repression and denying the gifts that are right below all that tumult. Instead, allowing that discomfort to express itself—through tears, wild dance, roaring, or however you choose—is the fastest way to transmute the energy and be able to witness the beauty in every experience.

I'm not implying that we have to spend loads of time brewing on difficult emotions (or, worse, to dump our unhappiness and pain onto others), but we do have a sacred right to explore it, to understand what it is trying to tell us about life and love.

When I was growing up, I was often told to smile, to not be sad, to "think positive". I was a super melancholy child, so this was always hard for me. To "put on a good face" when I was feeling so much pain and discomfort. I didn't understand why I couldn't just stare out the car window and cry about everything and nothing.

The depth of my feelings, even at that age, made the people around me uncomfortable. So, like many of us, I was taught to suppress anything that didn't "look" happy. As an adult, I had to give myself permission, over and over, to *feel*. And even when those feelings morphed into guilt and shame for not being happy, I allowed myself to feel that too. As I consistently practiced this acceptance of what I'd labeled as "wrong" for so long, those feeling-sensations began to morph again into a kind of blissful watching of the shifting tides within me, and I no longer had to judge any of them. I began to understand that if I would just let them have their turn, they would turn into something else. *Ahhh,* freedom. And the happiness that lives in trusting yourself that much.

THE "I'LL BE HAPPY WHEN..." TRAP

Another way we block the joyful freedom of experiencing life with openness and trust is when we decide that happiness is the result of something "outside" of us. That if only we *had* this or that, if only we *were* this or that, everything would be great. We can't blame ourselves for this. We're bombarded daily with messages of: *Unhappy? Just use this product/service/system, and you'll find happiness/love/serenity.* Argh. So we buy the thing, hire the "expert", sign up for the newsletter... someone, something, *anything* to take away the existential ache, to give us "success" or to "quick fix" our way to happiness.

But here's the truth: If that someone or something isn't pointing you back to *yourself*, then it won't work. You'll just keep spinning outward, in a dizzying spell of searching for what was always yours in the first place. The only one who has your answers is you... just like Dorothy in *The Wizard of Oz*, who had the way back home all along—she just needed the witch's pointing to remember.

Once you are aware of this truth and are wary of anyone telling you they have your answers, you will also want to keep an eye on the ego because it can get in the way with the same story: *Just as soon as you have the car, the title, the position, the overflowing bank account, then you can rest. Then you'll have the peace, the love, the joy.* As Jim Carrey once said, "How tricky is this ego that it would tempt us with the promise of something we already possess?" He was talking about immortality. But the same goes for happiness, or anything else for that matter.

Now, don't get me wrong. Personally, I'm a big fan of the ego. My ego lets me get up on stage and deliver a message with the conviction that only a "personality" could present. It's what "acts the part" when I'm in a Fortune 500 boardroom so that I can convince a CEO, CMO, or CFO of the right course of action. But my ego is just that—a personality that I have created to share inspiration, guidance, and support—an instrument to guide others back to the truth that was in them all along.

When our ego is in service in this way, there is no end to the heights we can reach. And the heights themselves are no longer important. Aligning your ego—or human expression—to the divine truths in you is like a constant spontaneous enlightenment that does not rely on anything or anyone outside of you for its fulfilment.

KEEP COMING BACK TO YOURSELF

There are going to be moments when you don't feel happy. And you don't know how to give yourself permission to feel that way either. That's the truth. And it's okay. Another truth is that another wave of joy and liberation will hit you after that, and maybe permission will be hard then too. That's also okay.

Years ago, I can't remember where, I read something about everyone having a kind of "happiness set point." Like a thermostat, you would keep going back to that point, so you couldn't get that much happier (or sadder, I guess). Many times I've also heard that happiness is a choice, and we all know how annoying it is to hear *that* when we're feeling like crap.

I'm not big on either one of those theories. First, I believe that happiness is not as straightforward as we make it sound. Happiness can be found in the most unlikely places. The darkest corners of our pain can reveal the greatest gifts, an almost ecstatic awareness of life's beauty. Second, the real choice we have is where we're putting our attention and thought-action energy. So, if I'm deciding that this or that thing is "bad" and giving myself all sorts of reasons why that is so, then I've missed the boat. Instead, if I'm exploring it with open, loving curiosity, I can sail life's seas with less effort and greater ease.

When I first sat down to write this chapter, I was feeling unhappy. I didn't have an "excuse" for feeling that way—but I didn't have to have a *reason* to go into the feeling. What I wrote was, "I don't feel happy at the moment. And that's okay. I know the tide will soon turn, if I just let the unhappiness have its turn." As I continued to sit with it, I realized that the chemistry in my body was off. I felt it as a kind of heaviness between my gut and my solar plexus, occasionally traveling up in waves to my heart. I also felt blocked in my throat, as if some energy or expression couldn't make it through. All of this came as a kind of spontaneous understanding, and I then received the prompt of how to shift it.

Staying present with these feeling-sensations that I was labeling as "unhappiness" allowed the next impulse to arise: MOVE. I became aware that I needed to get up and dance or shake or gently stretch my body. That kind of deep listening always provides the answer that allows us to adjust our perception so we can feel safe and continue moving in the direction we've claimed for ourselves. It also reveals another truth: The fastest way to change your psychological state is to change your physical state—the way you're using your body.

So, if you need a quick reset, take a break now and invite your body to play. Experience the joy of being here now in the physical.

BOUNDARIES, BABY, BOUNDARIES

As you step more and more into play and the connection that arises from presence with yourself, your emotions, and your body, you might find you need some new boundaries. Boundaries with yourself and with others.

Almost twenty years ago, I remember reading a statistic that the average American was exposed to somewhere near three thousand advertisements per day—mostly through television and print media. Again, this was *twenty years ago.* My head spins to imagine how many ads pass across all our screens today. No matter where you live, it's likely that you're bombarded by media. And most of it is saying you're not good enough, smart enough, pretty enough, thin enough, whatever enough. You're just not enough…unless you buy the solution they're selling.

Well, I'm not buying. I call BS. And I also call a timeout. Enough already of the not-enoughness.

If we want to avoid comparison traps and the constant deluge of targeted ads, we have to set some boundaries. We have to do what we'd do with a young child: limit exposure. Since we've already covered minimizing the time dedicated to *other people's priorities,* I'll avoid belaboring the point here. But just notice, when you're scrolling and scrolling: how do you feel? Do you feel connected, alive, and joyful? Or do you feel drained, frustrated, and scattered? If it's the latter, experiment with easing up and returning to the search for beauty and lightness within.

Another boundary we sometimes need to set is around what we tell ourselves. I once heard Deepak Chopra say, "Every cell in your body is eavesdropping on your inner dialogue." What are you telling yourself about yourself, dear reader? Are they messages that reinforce your innate right to happiness and inner peace? If not, boundaries need to be erected there too.

This is coming from someone who's always been her own harshest critic. It's taken years for me to pull out those thought weeds and replace them with the beautiful thought flowers that populate my life now. Setting this boundary of what you will *not* tell yourself or believe about yourself is the hardest boundary of all because it requires reversing what for most of us has been a lifetime of beating ourselves up. But you are the only one with 24-hour access to your own psyche, and if you don't make a firm decision to guard that precious gateway, no one will.

All of these boundaries are a kind of detox to ease off the social addictions to distraction, comparison, and not-enoughness so you can begin to restore your natural state of wholeness. Eventually, you come to a place where boundaries are no longer necessary. There is an equanimity in your being that, just like with the farmer from the previous chapter, welcomes all visitors, watching them come and go without attachment or resistance.

Let's look a bit deeper at how this inner restoration can start to take place.

RESTORING AND REPLENISHING YOURSELF

Have you ever had a leak in your house and you put a bucket under to catch the water while you figured out the problem or called someone to figure it out for you? Did you notice how quickly the bucket fills? Maybe you had to empty that first bucket while putting another in its place, to keep catching the leak?

When you look at one drop of water, it doesn't seem like something serious. But all those single drops fill a bucket, fast. One thought. One behavior. One time. Same thought. Same behavior. Next time. Over and over. The "house" of your body and mind is flooded with the insidious drops of anger or fear or anxiety, and now you're drowning in the character those thoughts and behaviors have created.

But what if instead of continuing to race around collecting all those gushing leaks, you decide to mend the cracks and recycle the collected water? It's a lot of work. You have to decide if your happiness is worth it, or if you prefer to just keep the "quick fix" routine active in your life. The buckets you've been using and the temporary relief of draining the water let you forget for a moment that you're leaking—you're draining your energy. You have to decide if you are willing to restore the house of your body and mind and go straight to the source of the problem.

There are three distinct, yet simultaneous actions we must take to restore and replenish ourselves:

1. Mend the source of the leak.
2. Recycle the water we've collected.
3. Remove the buckets so we can freely move around our mind-body home once and for all.

In this metaphor, the water leak is the energy leak. The cracks are the traumas in our psyche that were never addressed. The buckets are what we use to avoid dealing with the cracks.

Let's look first at the buckets themselves because they are the easiest to identify. Your "buckets" are anything you're using to *fill so you don't have to feel.* This could be an excess of work, food, alcohol, or whatever helps you avoid dealing with what led you to them in the first place. The ways we hide from ourselves and our pain are many, and again, they are symptomatic of the bigger problem. Whatever your buckets, give thanks for the ways they have kept you from completely drowning, and resolve to recycle that water so it can feed a new *cyclical* ecosystem (more on that in a second).

First, let's look at mending the cracks themselves—the original wounds that were never healed and those from which energy is still seeping.

These original cracks could have been extreme, like abuse in childhood, or they could have been something relatively mild, like not being accepted by your peers when you were in grade school. Whatever the original pain, the result was the same: You tried to protect yourself from it. You gave your mind and body the job of doing whatever it could to deal with it and try to ensure that it wouldn't happen again. Now, if you're reading this, you are ready to allow that original trauma to dissolve, to hand it over to that great power within you that is standing by, ready for your healing.

Luckily, we don't have to be aware of what the original trauma was in order to heal it, which is great news, because most of us can't remember how or why we fell into certain pain responses. All we have to do is *be* with the resulting sensation (pre-behavior) when it arises and begin to ask some questions—get curious and *stay with it until it can change form and go elsewhere.*

Let me give an example. Let's say an excess of food or alcohol is your go-to (the bucket that collects the energy drain) to avoid dealing with the cracks. You notice that instead of eating and drinking for enjoyment and nourishment, you're consuming to numb and distract yourself. Once you recognize this pattern and decide you don't want it running your life and ruining your health, you're ready for something very simple, yet hard at first. You're ready to be with that trapped sensation for the time it takes for it to finally be able to move through you. What this means is that the moment the desire arises to fill in this way, you avoid rushing in to remedy the situation and instead you just sit and be with it. You get present, breathe, and notice what's happening. If you have the courage to do this, it will stop running your life.

All sorts of things will happen when you do this. You might start to cry. You might have flashes of insight or recollect something from your past. You might even notice, as I and my clients often have, that the desire to self-medicate will just vanish. It will go somewhere else. This is when you know you're mending that crack. The more you do this, the less energy leaks you will have in your system. The more you will be restoring the house of your body and mind. This is your new cyclical ecosystem.

Now you're ready to recycle all that dirty water you've been collecting. The earth loves it when we give that all back as a kind of compost for new life. Actual physical release is the best way I've found for this—shake out your whole body, go for a run or a brisk walk in the woods, dance your heart out. Any way you want to use your body as a means of release will work! Just keep doing it. Eventually you'll be ready to get rid of the protection itself—the buckets, which were only ever an illusion of protection anyway. You'll be ready to put them away and walk around life with an open and trusting heart.

This new approach to life will make the thought directing/redirecting process we looked at in the last chapter that much easier. You will have decided that freedom and happiness are the priority. And the new thought and behavioral patterns that arise will illuminate the temple of your home and your heart.

SIGNALING YOUR BODY IN NEW WAYS

When you begin to heal the energy leaks and commit to new thought and behavioral patterns in these ways, you are also directly changing *who you are*.

Imagine for a moment having an infinite library at your disposal. Every book in this library represents a different life experience or potential that is available to you. All you have to do is choose the book that matches what you want to be and experience. Only, instead of taking out new books (trying on new potentials), you keep grabbing the same book every day. This book says you are Joe Smith; you live in Maryland; you're a lawyer; your best friend is Gloria, and your girlfriend is Sam. This is *your* book, and it defines you. You're not all that happy with it, though. Your job is unsatisfying; you don't like where you live; and your relationships need work. This is the story. It's hard and uncomfortable. But it's *your* story, your book.

Now, what if you decide one day that you're going to leave that book right where it is, and you're going to go look for a new book, or a sequel that provides resolution and evolution. You stop grabbing for the old story —you stop signaling your body and mind in ways that reinforce its contents. You are ready to reinvent your life. You are ready to be free, to play, to be happy. This is when the restoration we discussed above becomes imperative.

When you commit to repairing the home of your body and mind, you can start experimenting with leaving it all together. After all, it's not the truth of who you are. You are not the home. You are merely living in the home. Just as you are not the books. You are the one behind or in front of all the books, experiencing the adventures they hold. You can choose a new adventure.

I've studied multiple findings of people instantly changing their physical realities, including their appearance, when they began to embrace a new idea of themselves, and I share some of these studies in my lectures and talks around the world. But I probably wouldn't have fully believed these studies if I hadn't experienced these phenomena first hand. In my talks, I sometimes show a picture of myself from ten years ago, and I always receive a shocked response from the audience. *That couldn't possibly be you*, they gape.

The truth is, that image isn't *me*. It's a projection of my consciousness at that time. And happiness—just like beauty or truth—is a state of consciousness, a state of awareness. This mind-body home we're living in is temporary. So why not recognize this now and begin to play around with creating new versions of ourselves?

When we do, we open to a love that is beyond all understanding. This love is the subject of our next chapter.

CHAPTER 10

Be Loved

This might be the most difficult permission to grant ourselves: Permission to be loved, lovable, and worthy of love. And yet, it is the one on which all the others rest. Perhaps unlike the others, it's less about "permission" and more about *recognition*—seeing yourself, your nature, clearly. Because this is all that you are: love, loved, lovable, worthy of all the love.

When you came into this world, you knew that you didn't have to do or attain anything to deserve love. You knew you were inherently worthy of it all. Giving yourself permission to be loved is coming back to this knowing that has always lived in you.

⸻

Growing up in a family of five kids, I learned to conflate love with attention; the desire to be seen and worthy of attention informed a lot of my behavior. *We all want to be seen.* Not seen in a "Hey, hey look at me!" kind of way, but in a true "I see you" kind of way. *I see you beyond all the masks you thought you had to wear. I see the truth of love in you.*

Funny enough, the word "person" comes from *persona*, which was the mask worn in ancient Greek theater. When we consider this origin, we are confronted with the staggering realization that we are all wearing masks—acting out roles in an epic saga. What's behind or under all those masks? What happens if we dare to remove them, if we take a bow and leave the character behind us?

What happens is we find Love. We touch that truth within us that knows *only* love, that is immune to concepts of judgment or guilt or fear. We touch the truth that watches and smiles upon all that is. This truth knows that all that is, and all you are, is perfect.

Daring to connect with this truth is frightening. It means you have to leave behind all your ideas of rightdoing and wrongdoing, all the masks you've carefully crafted to help yourself feel safe, all the clever means and ways you've devised to appear as somebody "special" or "important". We have to let it all go because everything we build to find this love blocks it from us.

The irony is, once you are ready to give it all up, you get it. You get the kind of love you craved all along. The kind of love that can never leave or forsake you. The kind of love that drops you to your knees in awe and wonder and fills you with an ever-expanding sense of gratitude for all that is. *Because this is the truth of what you are.*

PLAYING A NEW GAME

So, how can we embrace this truth of love within us? How can we know it? Especially if we're disappointed in ourselves or if we're all tangled up in some story about not being lovable, or that we have to be different than we currently are in order to merit love? How do we access this inner love light when it seems like it's all snuffed out?

We merely need to recognize that under all the conditioning that has convinced us we need to have more, do more, be more…under all that, the love light is still there. Once we remember this "love light", we go searching for it. We devote ourselves to it. And in the process, we deny all that is not true to it. Layer after layer, we drop the story that has blocked the light of this truth.

Every time another strand of "not-enoughness" emerges, we drop it; we let it melt into the brightness of our future. Every time we feel ourselves pulling up protection from judgment or criticism—from ourselves or others—we let it fall back down. We decide we're not going to perform the role that keeps the show going. Instead, **we keep bringing our attention back to the zero point field of love within.**

Healing in this way requires intense focus and effort at first. We are turning a massive ship around. We must turn the helm slowly and deliberately. Decision after decision, we disinvest our attention from the direction we've been heading in, and we reinvest our attention and energy in the direction we're turning toward: Love. This will be difficult until it becomes the default.

Let's look first at what we're no longer accepting, what we must commit to turning our attention and energy away from...

Most of us grow up questioning our lovability. Even if you had an emotionally healthy household (and, let's face it, a lot of us didn't), society still delivers this message fairly early on. We are taught that our lovability and worthiness are based on some sort of standard of excellence—a standard we can only chase and never fully attain. The average school teaches us that our worthiness is based mostly on our ability to perform well academically and/or physically (sports). Our peers look to our "style" or our attitude to determine our likeability. Our guardians, teachers, coaches, and peers can punish or promote us based on our ability to perform.

While we're getting beat up by family (however well intentioned) and school teachers and peers (however well intentioned), we start the worst beating of all: *We begin beating up ourselves.* We begin the inner sabotage. And our inner doubting that we are inherently worthy of love is the most insidious of all. Because it's not coming from "out there"; it's coming from "in here". Hence, we can no longer separate ourselves from it. Our identity becomes inextricably linked. It's now our baseline and is reflected back from everything and everyone. Game over.

That's when it's time to play a new game.

It's kind of a sneaky one because, rather than all at once, we redirect our thought-action energy bit by bit so that we're slipping this new way of being right by our conscious mind, undetected. Like the ship, if all the weight/momentum was behind a single-pointed direction (not worthy of love unless…), we have to begin with *subtle* course corrections. We slowly shift this core belief around lovability.

Often when people start this kind of work, they tell me, "Hey, Cort, I've been at it a couple of weeks now, and it's not working." My response is invariably, "Well, how long did it take you to get where you are now?" You have to acknowledge how much effort and energy and attention you've expended up to this point in reinforcing whatever you believe about yourself and your "reality". Creating new beliefs, and hence a new reality for yourself, takes time at first. Keep trusting. This new (virtuous) thought-action cycle will eventually become automatic.

REMEMBER: IT'S JUST A FALSE ELECTRICAL IMPULSE

When the "not worthy" or "not enough" or "not love-able" thoughts strike, know this:

1. Thoughts like these are electrical impulses that are in the collective mind around us. That does not make them true. It makes them a pattern of consciousness that we have the opportunity to release and transmute *at will*.

2. In order to release and transform these thought/feeling patterns/impulses:

   a) First, you have to acknowledge the thought itself. This might sound simple, but it's actually the hardest part at the beginning. The reason it's the hardest is that if we've accepted these kinds of thoughts for a long time, they begin to feel so familiar that we believe *we are the thought*. So first, just become aware: "Ah, *there's that thought.*"

   b) From this place of noticing, we can then recognize that it is only a thought and it is *not true*. Literally, we tell ourselves: *"This is only a thought; it is not true."* (For evidence of this, simply consider how many times in the past a fearful or uncomfortable thought that occurred to you was false.)

c) Once you've singled out this kind of thought and exposed it for what it is—an untrue electrical impulse—you are in a position to consciously *choose* the truth. The truth is love, joy, peace. Whatever you want to call it, the truth is innately clear, because **the truth *feels* good.** It's not a fleeting kind of good, but a lasting *ahhhh* that inspires expansion.

We can't do this through the mind alone. Please, please: *Do not try to force your mind to think a different thought.* You will never win that game. Instead, simply relax; notice the thought, without resistance or clinging; and then gently shift your attention and awareness to the love light within you. You will *sense* this loving intelligence within. You will feel it. You're not thinking about it or trying to get to it. Because YOU ARE IT. The mind is not involved.

As you also continue to use your body as an instrument to release what you don't want to hold on to mentally or emotionally, as we saw in the previous chapter, it will become increasingly easier to exchange old thought patterns for new ones whenever you are ready to start using the mind again.

With this kind of release, we are not resisting the thought or the bodily reaction to the thought. (Again, that will only reinforce it.) We only have to bring our loving awareness to what is happening in the body—to the felt sensations. Are we contracted somewhere in our body? If so, where? If we breathe into that sense of contraction and really stay with it, then it will transmute its energy within seconds. When freed, that energy will eventually transform into a sense of expansion or lightness.

WHEN WE REMOVE THE MASKS

The more you practice giving up whatever is in the way of love, through these waves of relaxing and releasing that we're talking about, the more potentials become available to you.

Let's go back for a moment to the concept of the masks—the persona, the character. *When you realize that you are not the character is also when you will begin to identify less and less with the performance.*

A couple of things will happen if you dare to become aware like this of how you've been hiding from yourself.

The first is that you will want to remove the mask, the costume, the guise. Now, you can imagine what would happen in any great performance if one of the characters decides to remove his costume. The other performers would become highly uncomfortable. You're naked. And it's freaking everyone out. "Put your costume back on!" would be the explicit or implicit directive.

If you can stand in that white fire and let it purify you, if you can trust more in yourself than in the initial reactions of others, if you can keep returning to the light and love within, then you will be a mastermind. At that point, you can put on any costume of your choosing. You can be the director, the producer, the lead actor…any and every role…all the while, totally aware that you are none of them (and all of them at the same time). It becomes fun. You are playing. (In the greatest play ever.)

As you play like this, dancing around the stage, another phenomenon will occur. You will become less enamored with the performance and more excited by the one who is behind the whole show.

Because you're not who you think you are. You're just not. And, yet, you're potentially *everything* you think you are.

THE COURAGE TO STOP PERFORMING

Two days ago I was speaking to a singer-songwriter friend of mine and telling him about my music. On and off for a few years now, I've been writing songs (mostly snippets of songs) and playing along with vocals and my guitar, occasionally also with my piano. I don't really know what I'm doing and haven't had much formal training. But I love it.

Or I guess I should say that I just recently rediscovered my love for it.

———

Four years ago, I wrote my first song, called "The Dolphin" (even if the word dolphin isn't anywhere in the lyrics). There I was, lingering on a comfy couch in a friend's music studio in the south of France. I was totally relaxed, listening to my friends jam on their Fenders, while I was jamming on the love within me and its desire to create and love more. This song just came through me. Line by line without any "work". It was perfect.

I was so excited by it that I recorded it and sent it to some of my close friends around the world. My non-professional, yet very musical friends loved it. They said they were listening to it over and over again and couldn't get enough. My professional music friends, on the other hand, said it was good but that it needed work. A few comments on my not-so-technical skills, and I shrank.

I started thinking of my music in terms of a "performance" and as something I had to get "right"—a shift from *feeling* to *forcing*. The joy was gone. My guitar went untouched. Sometimes I'd pick it up to practice what I was told I needed to "work on", but that's what it felt like: work.

Then, during the writing of this book, something magical happened. Opening to the love within me that wanted to share what you're reading (or listening to) reminded me that what other people think of it is none of my business. My business is connecting with that love light and letting it shine through me. That's all. That's all I have to "do". And that's when the music started coming through again.

Then came the greatest gift: My daughter Gaia asked me to play for her. She had never asked me to do this before. In fact, the times she'd heard me playing (or, rather, I should say "performing") in the past, she promptly asked me to stop. She didn't like it. Once again, she knew what I didn't. She knew I wasn't *playing*; she knew I was *performing*. It was forced. This time, when she listened, we were connecting through the music because it was real. We could both feel it. And enjoy it. We were in the love of it. This is the truth in you, and it doesn't need to be demonstrated; it only needs to be recognized. By you.

It's easy to slip back out of this awareness. Just go back in.

Funny enough, right after I played four or five of my songs for Gaia, I had her listen to a friend's recording—one I knew was technically "perfect". I liked the song, but she immediately scrunched up her nose after the first verse and didn't want to listen anymore, saying, "Yours are much better, Mama." I couldn't agree or disagree with that. All I could do was marvel at her innate connection with play and love.

Most of us get lost in the performance, never to re-emerge. Don't let this be you.

DON'T WORRY, YOU HAVE A LOT OF HELP

None of what I'm proposing is overnight quick-fix stuff. (Oh, how I wish it were.)

It's the daily remembrance of love in you. The daily remembrance of light in you. The daily remembrance of God in you. Until this becomes where you live from…

Grace. It's always there. It's waiting for you to connect with It.

You don't have to figure it out. Also because you can't. Just let go. Trust. Keep going back.

Anytime you're in a spin, just sit or move and talk (literally) with this loving intelligence. Ask for the healing, ask for the opening, ask for the TRUST.

Wait for the answers. Action what you can.

It's so simple. We just have to remember to do it.

And while you're at it: Play around with *handing it all over*—the moment those sensations of control or contraction or anger or frustration or fear come in, open your fingers and hand it off to the Divine. Say, "Here, You take it. Thank You."

When you're not feeling loved or lovable, *pray*. Ask to come home to this love. What you'll find on the other side of those feelings is beauty…the exquisite beauty of it all. The tears, the fears, the pain, even these you will experience with joy.

Sit back. Let the love come to you. *There is no need to seek what is already there.* Everywhere. In and all around you.

Keep dropping the masks. Let go. Open up. Shine the light of who you are on every experience.

This loving intelligence that lives within you will reveal everything you need to know to become who you are ready to be. When you feel it, it will bend your knees. And you'll know that love—like beauty, truth, and happiness—is an inner job. That will then be what you radiate outward and invite back in.

Opening up to this loving intelligence and allowing it to take over will give you the greatest permission of all: permission to be YOU.

Be You

Behind all the permission you give yourself to believe, to change your mind, to do what you love and get rich doing it, to have fun, to opt out of what doesn't serve you, and to design your life the way you want it, to be confident, happy, and loved…behind all that, *you are.*

It's time to believe. *You get to decide what you're going to believe.* And if you hold that new belief of yourself with conviction, it will begin to define your reality. Fix your attention on empowering, uplifting questions and witness how quickly people, situations, circumstances and events arise to meet and reinforce your upgraded vision.

Anywhere along the way, feel free to change your mind, adjusting your beliefs and behaviors to suit the highest potential you can imagine for yourself and others. Notice the difference between when changing your mind and adopting a new direction feels *expansive* versus when it is based in fear; rise to meet your expansion and allow your fears to melt away, as you stay true to the *you* you're becoming.

Keep connecting to what you love to do, how you want to spend the majority of your waking hours. Even if it feels scary at first, you do get to do what you love. That's why you're here—it's the space in the puzzle you're meant to fill. And when you really love what you're doing, others will love it too. There are about eight billion of us here, and you are meant to reach and inspire as many of us as can benefit from your gifts and talents.

Let that inspiration lead you to all the riches your heart desires, as you focus on cultivating wealth inside you—a wealth of joy, of love, of peace. Align your beliefs with this new picture and understanding of wealth. Remember that where love is, money is, and that no one else can do you. Gratitude will speed everything along and astonish you with its compounding power.

Remember to play. You're spinning around a star on a ball of dirt in the middle of infinite space, so there's no need to take any of it too seriously. Laugh. Have fun. That's when you'll have the biggest breakthroughs. Decide to enjoy it all, even (maybe especially) the sticky, messy parts. Creating from fun will ease your efforts, relax your nervous system, and begin to reveal endless potentials to you.

Aligning with playful creation requires a break from all the noise. So give yourself permission to opt out of anything that feels icky or is otherwise unrelated to your vision of yourself and the beliefs that reinforce that vision. Safeguard your morning and evening times, using these precious portals to "reprogram" your mind and body into ever expanding states of peace and connection. When you're less distracted, deluded, and stressed by external stimuli and by the interests of others, you will find a focus and softness that allows you to design a life you love.

As you begin to live by design, rather than by default, your whole being will reorganize to adapt to the knowing that life's every event is supporting who you're becoming. You will anchor into and exude *real* confidence—a deep trust in yourself and the Force that powers you and everything else. It will become increasingly easier to train your mind to release judgment, to relax into inspired action, and to stay open to surprise and wonder.

This is when you will know happiness. You will sense the joy in life's every wave. It won't always "look" happy and that won't matter to you anymore. Your happiness will be independent of what occurs outside of you. You will discover that happiness, just like beauty or truth, is a state of consciousness, a state of awareness, and you will live in this ecstatic awareness as you continually restore and replenish your inner and outer reserves.

Very naturally, you will be shedding whatever has been in the way of you connecting to and knowing the love that is within and all around you. All messages of not being/having/doing enough will fade into inspired thought-action, as you recognize the truth of who and what you are: love, loved, lovable, worthy of all the love. This formless truth will then inform the form in new, bright, and beautiful ways.

It won't always feel good. It's not supposed to. The waves of contraction and surrender are how growth happens. Where you're going is very different from where you've been. And it means having to continually let go of how you thought it would look.

Keep moving (literally!) throughout all this unraveling and reforming. Keep advancing, like the pawn on a chessboard that, despite all odds, makes it to the other side, where it can transform into a queen—with the freedom to go where she wants.

Let this writing be an invitation for you to go wherever you need to go, to change form as many times as is needed until you understand that you are *not* the form, to remember the truth behind and beyond all of it. You will have then unlocked what Elisabeth Browning calls "the imprisoned splendor." Your presence will be the fulcrum, your shared gifts will be the lever, and you will move the world.

If any part of this book resonates as truth with you, highlight it and return to it until it becomes your own. Most people stay on the surface. They finish a book and rush on to the next one—wildly searching for answers from outside. I urge you to use this book as a way to go deep *inside*. Let it guide you back, over and over, to *you*. It will be boring at first, since our brains are trained to prefer novelty. But if you can stick with it like this, you will go deeper and deeper, into a place where you will no longer need any book or any external source to tell you what you knew all along, what only you ever had access to: the joy and love and peace and wonder that has always been *within* you, that *is* you.

I bow to a master,

C.

PS: *Thank you so much for being YOU. I love you for it.*

PPS: *I'd love to stay in touch. Please connect on Instagram (@cortneymcdermott) or through CORTINC.com where you can find a free mini meditation to relax into the concepts covered in this book.*

Acknowledgments

Thank you from the top, bottom, and middle of my heart to everyone who gave me permission when I couldn't give it to myself…

This book wouldn't be possible without my brothers and sisters, the blood ones and the ones life chose for me. Thank you Dave, Ace, Ginny, and Doug for showing up in spades whenever I've needed you. And to the entire McDermott-Shonk-Sully Clan for being so cool.

A very special thank you to Giulia Traverso, who double checked the science and logic throughout this manuscript—you're a godsend. Super props to Jamison McDermott who set me straight on the title from the beginning and provided insight throughout. And heartfelt thanks to Sunaina Narang and the whole Wisdom House Publishing Team for keeping me on track and pushing me to go deeper when I didn't want to.

Endless thanks also to Tatiana Arias for being a lighthouse to thousands, including me; to Elisabet Alfstad for grounding me in this world in your otherworldly way;

to Dominic Alie for teaching me so much about music and life; to Sally Bell for our Marco Polo sessions and your unmatchable intelligence; to Valentina Hernandez for your wit, kindness, and ability to solve any problem, and to the other members of my Bassano crew—Gabriel Hernandez and Giulia Scomazzon—for helping me through one of the toughest transitions in my life; to Sameera Suri for confirming over twenty years ago that I'd be a writer; to Izabela Hamilton for your contagious smile, humor, and playfulness; to Lauren Sokol for your brilliance and mad improv skills; to Elaine Musselman for your strength and healing leadership; to Liza Leiss for inspiring me and so many others with your golden footprints; to Luca Pauletti, who has so lovingly supported me and my dreams throughout the years; and to Maria Angélica Dávila for your generous heart and curandera spirit. And thank you, again, to Dana and Gaia, without whom I wouldn't be here.

Infinite gratitude to God—my partner in all this, and to You, dear reader... I love you.

Thank You

Thank you for reading my book!

Before you go, can you please leave a quick review on Amazon?

All you have to do is scroll down our Amazon listing where reviews are, and select "write a customer review." Even just a couple of words will really help spread the word.

My dream is that this book can be a kind of portal to your truth, and that we can all live confident, happy, full lives.

Thanks again. Connecting with you means the world to me.

Check out
Cortney McDermott's first bestselling book.

Change Starts Within You:

Cultivating Confidence and Empowering Transformation is an empowering self-help book. Cortney guides readers on a transformative journey towards developing self-confidence and initiating personal change. Through insightful wisdom and practical strategies, the book inspires readers to embark on a path of self-discovery and empowers them to take charge of their lives.

Buy a copy of the book on
www.amazon.com

Notes